HUXLEY

BRAVE NEW WORLD
AND
BRAVE NEW WORLD REVISITED

Revised by WILSON F. ENGEL, Ph.D.

ABOUT COLES NOTES

COLES NOTES have been an indispensible aid to students on five continents since 1948.

COLES NOTES are available for a wide range of individual literary works. Clear, concise explanations and insights are provided along with interesting interpretations and evaluations.

Proper use of COLES NOTES will allow the student to pay greater attention to lectures and spend less time taking notes. This will result in a broader understanding of the work being studied and will free the student for increased participation in discussions.

COLES NOTES are an invaluable aid for review and exam preparation as well as an invitation to explore different interpretive paths.

COLES NOTES are written by experts in their fields. It should be noted that any literary judgement expressed herein is just that — the judgement of one school of thought. Interpretations that diverge from, or totally disagree with any criticism may be equally valid.

COLES NOTES are designed to supplement the text and are not intended as a substitute for reading the text itself. Use of the NOTES will serve not only to clarify the work being studied, but should enhance the reader's enjoyment of the topic.

ISBN 0-7740-3245-6

Manufactured by Webcom Limited
Cover finish: Webcom's Exclusive **Duracoat**

CONTENTS

Aldous Huxley: Life and Works

Aldous Leonard Huxley (1894-1963) was born in Surrey, England, and died in Los Angeles, California. He had the kind of liberal education described by his famous grandfather Thomas Henry Huxley:

> That man, I think, has had a liberal education who has been so trained in youth that his body is the ready servant of his will, and does with ease and pleasure all the work that, as a mechanism, it is capable of; whose intellect is a clear, cold, logic engine, with all its parts of equal strength, and in smooth working order; ready, like a steam engine, to be turned to any kind of work, and spin the gossamers as well as forge the anchors of the mind; whose mind is stored with a knowledge of the great and fundamental truths of Nature and of the laws of her operations; one who, no stunted ascetic, is full of life and fire, but whose passions are trained to come to heel by a vigorous will, the servant of a tender conscience; who has learned to love all beauty, whether of Nature or of art, to hate all vileness, and to respect others as himself.

Aldous Huxley wrote a biography of his grandfather that was published in 1932, when *Brave New World* first appeared in print. Clearly he had a distinguished family behind him, and Eton and Balliol College, Oxford, rounded out his traditional education.

But Aldous Huxley was trained as an independent thinker as much by personal hardship and by his own seeking temperament as by his background. His book *The Art of Seeing* (1943) is a description of the methods by which he trained himself out of the crippling blindness of *keratitis punctata*. His edition of the letters of D.H. Lawrence (1933) shows his discipleship (if that is not too strong a word) to that radical thinker and novelist, to whom he is indebted for much of the material in *Brave New World*. Huxley wrote about how his physical blindness forced him to try to see — both what was visible and what was hidden — in everything. The vast range of his interests is reflected in his abundant output of writings.

1

Although Huxley was a dabbler in poetry, his first literary fame came from the publication of *Crome Yellow* (1921), a novel. This was followed by *Antic Hay* (1923), *Those Barren Leaves* (1925), *Point Counter Point* (1928) — considered his masterpiece by some critics — *Brave New World* (written 1931, published 1932), *Eyeless in Gaza* (1936), *After Many a Summer Dies the Swan* (1939), *Ape and Essence* (1948), *The Devils of Loudon* (1952), and *The Genius and the Goddess* (1955). Through his works can be traced an increasingly pessimistic view of the modern world. Novels were only part of his prolific output. In addition to the biography, the manual on vision, and the edition of Lawrence's letters mentioned above, Huxley also wrote numerous essays, plays, and two collections of poems.

Huxley visited Italy many times in the twenties and early thirties, where he saw D.H. Lawrence. In 1934 he visited Central America, and in 1937 he went to America, where he settled in California. His travel book *Beyond the Mexique Bay* (1934) grew out of his first trip. California then as now offered a fertile field of new and often shocking ideas, and Huxley avidly studied the currents – particularly religious currents – stirring there. Mainly on account of the immense popularity of *Brave New World*, he was a celebrity. The Foreword to the novel, republished in 1946, made clear that it was still a viable statement then. *Brave New World Revisited* (1958) alludes to Huxley's place among the foremost futurists in the world. He was clearly a defender of humanism, against the rising tide of the social science engineers.

For all of his disillusionment with the products of science in the mushrooming of technology, Huxley remained scientific in his approach to reality. Where he differed from the technicians was in his dependence, not on an uncritical acceptance of tradition, but on the integrity of his own mind. His experiments with life, vision, and drugs were based not only on what other people wrote, but on his own assessment of the experiences he had had. Huxley had an almost missionary drive to teach what he learned, and to associate his insights with humane values. Part of the appeal of *Brave New World* is its refusal to become totally cynical. Its playful wit is coupled with a refined sympathy for characters of all kinds.

Huxley married twice. His first wife, Maria Nys, bore him one son, Matthew; his second wife, Laura Archera, whom he married in 1956, wrote memoirs of him after he died.

Huxley's grandfather was a major force in English education, and took a stand for science against the forces of institutional religion. Aldous Huxley, like him, was a public, not a private, person. His influence on currents of thought in America in the fifties and sixties may never be fully traced. *Brave New World* has been for over fifty years a classic text for middle and high school, and even college. Huxley's tireless lecturing and writing complemented his book in warning society to be aware of its future. While his other novels require some effort on the reader's part to adapt to the time and situation, *Brave New World* still is readily accessible and has a message that speaks to us today.

After the appearance of *1984*, by George Orwell, in 1948, *Brave New World* came under attack as a false picture of the future, particularly by Orwell, who wrote, "it probably casts no light on the future" (see Selected Criticisms). Huxley defended the accuracy of his prophecy in *Brave New World Revisited*. It is a book of serious, moral essays, in which Huxley warns about the subtle threads that are beginning to bind mankind. In an age of "experts" it is easy to ignore the statements of those who see things whole. Huxley by 1958 was fighting the experts and the mass of people who believe only them.

Introduction to *Brave New World*

Huxley's *Brave New World* defies a perfect label. Generally it can be called a novel about utopia, a place that never was but might be. As such, its ancestry could be traced to Thomas More's *Utopia,* whose title means "good place" or "no place," or both. World literature is full of examples of utopian works and also dystopian works (those dealing with bad, as opposed to good, places), and because he was extremely well read Huxley knew most of these works intimately. But *Brave New World* is not much like any other work in this tradition. Its tone of comedy, including some outrageous and even irresponsible jabs at contemporary figures and taboos, lifts it out of this literary tradition that runs from More's *Utopia* to Edward Ballamy's *Looking Backward* (1888).

The farcical nature of Huxley's work is closely akin to the Classical tradition of the Satyr play or of the irreverent and often ribald comedies of the Greek, Aristophanes. The *Satyricon* of Petronius, a Roman satirist, may also have stimulated some of Huxley's incisive scenes and the disjointed structure of, say, the Savage's tour of London. Satire in this tradition was not broad or generous, and it did not aim to reform, but only to make fun of people. Yet Huxley's work does more than make fun, and through the whole book there is both sympathy and seriousness.

One example of Huxley's use of a darker and more tragical tradition is the important interview of Mond and the Savage in Chapter 17. The subject is religion, and the tone is very serious. In *Brave New World Revisited* Huxley mentions the interview between the Grand Inquisitor and Alyosha in Dostoevsky's *The Brothers Karamazov*, and he most likely had this dark interview in mind when he wrote his own. The end of *Brave New World* is tragical, and so such a bridge to seriousness would be warranted.

Less clear is Huxley's reliance on Shakespeare in *Brave New World*, because Shakespeare represents more a state of mind or an approach to reality than a source for specific scenes. Shakespeare is also a symbol of the literature which a now-illiterate people (in the novel) has relegated to obscurity. The "feely" *Three Weeks in a Helicopter,* a grotesque farce based very remotely on Shakespeare's *Othello*, belongs more to the

19th-century tradition of Shakespearean farce, than to Shakespeare. In that tradition, as a diversion for audiences viewing Shakespearean drama, horrid farces not unlike *Three Weeks* were performed just before or just after the genuine Shakespeare. But *Brave New World* depends more on its Shakespearean quotations than on its resemblance to Shakespearean plots. The exception proves the rule: John's "O brave new world" from Miranda's statement in *The Tempest* is trampled underfoot in disillusionment and despair.

Brave New World's status as a novel might also be challenged. It is very short and very disjointed in its structure. It might be called a novella, or short novel, since it is longer than a short story. But its scope is at the same time too large and too small. Its themes are epic and involve the entire destiny of the human race, but its cast of characters, their statures, and the complexity of plotting fall short of the epic tradition. One might even say that the work operates more like one of Huxley's symbolist poems, using only the barest details to imply a vast order with vast meaning.

Clearly *Brave New World* is a didactic work — we are meant to learn something from reading it. Yet it is wholly different from the often tedious essays in *Brave New World Revisited*. Just what is to be learned is problematic. Is Mustapha Mond's pronouncement on God's necessary absence from the modern world the new gospel? Are we really to choose only between Malpais and 26th (or, if you will, 7th) century London? Is the course of humankind determined to bring the world to this impasse, or can another way be found? Clearly Huxley has written an often frivolous work, but his intent is not frivolous at all.

Part of the fun in *Brave New World* derives from its phenomenal variety — poetry, song, fantastic details, the changing landscapes, future history, the variations on themes in the distant society. Huxley plays on a full range of emotional effects also — pure farce, moral discourse, bathos, comic reversal, religious ritual, and tragedy combine with melodrama, romance, and description. The vitality of specific scenes, shifting from mood to mood in rapid succession, holds the interest at a high pitch, in a continual expectation of something new. Perhaps the most compressed and interesting — even most memorable — sequence in the book is the visit to the Savage

Reservation. That one part of the book could have been many hundreds of pages long. Instead, by compression, use of symbolic detail, anecdote, and powerful, mythic action, a world is implied in a few words. Compressed even more ruthlessly, the entire novel might become a blood brother to T.S. Eliot's *Wasteland*, except that Eliot's lapses into farce are carefully guarded and limited to a few contexts.

Brave New World is not a poem, but perhaps the best reading of it would begin with the premise that it is, for Huxley has structured his novel more like a poem than the standard novel. Notice that the very middle of the book involves the discovery by the Savage of the works of Shakespeare, that the first nine chapters involve the discovery of the Savage, and that the last nine chapters involve the Savage's interaction and progressive disillusionment with the Brave New World. Many scenes in the novel are meant to be compared and contrasted, for example the ones involving whips or Malthusian belts or "feelies" or mobs. The whole work is laced together with references to *soma* and happiness, or to Shakespeare and pain. It is as if Huxley deliberately set out to establish relationships that are all imperfect, for to pretend to perfection would be to share the mentality that defines the Brave New World.

As an example of the structure of *Brave New World*, take Huxley's use of geography. The largest portion of the earth's land mass belongs to the Brave New World, and even the other regions are carefully controlled by it. The Savage Reservation seems to be opposite to the Brave New World, yet in many respects the two regions are intimately related, as though they have long-forgotten connections. The dance of the *Penitentes* of Acoma is directly related to the (to us) farcical dance to "Orgy-porgy" at the Solidarity Service in the Brave New World. But a third region, much more secret than the Savage Reservation, also belongs to the earth — the penal islands, where enemies of the state are sent as a last resort. Just what they are like and how people interact there are left to the imagination. Exile is very much like death, as Mond grimly implies.

Huxley has formulated his new world around symbols — from the colour-coded dress of its Alpha-through-Epsilon populace, to the functional buildings in the landscape, to the drug symbols — from *soma* to V.P.S. The savage world has similar symbols, like the whip and John's eagle and the mesa itself. These symbols are natural for a symbolist poet, but the reader must understand that Huxley has packed his powerful images with meaning, in order to grasp the novel's larger purpose.

Thus *Brave New World* has antecedents as science fiction — even more than are explored above — but it is also a product of its time and the background of the man who wrote it.

Plot Summary

The Director of Hatcheries and Conditioning is introducing a group of new students to the Central London Hatchery and Conditioning Centre. They observe the process by which eggs are fertilized, embryos are engineered (according to their future class in society), toddlers are conditioned, and children are indoctrinated in their appropriate class's attitudes by sleep-teaching. Humans are shaped as Alphas, Betas, Gammas, Deltas, or Epsilons. No mothers, fathers or families are involved in the process; everything is scientifically managed on a world scale.

The group is surprised by Mustapha Mond, the World Controller for Western Europe, who tells them about the way things were before the time of Ford, and how events led up to the enlightened present age. While he speaks, the day shift is released from work and men and women speak of the pleasures that await them that evening. Henry Foster and Lenina Crowne play obstacle golf, eat at his place, go to a cabaret, and then make love. Bernard Marx spends the evening commiserating with his friend Helmholtz Watson. Bernard has trouble fitting in with his society. Even at Solidarity Service he has trouble achieving the ecstasy everyone else finds easily.

When he finally is out with Lenina Crowne, Bernard Marx wants to share some of his feelings with her, but she does not understand his desire for solitude, and at last he conforms, taking soma and taking her to bed. But he is uneasy at their next meeting and says dangerous things. They plan to go to the Savage Reservation together, and Bernard stops by the Director's office to get his signature permitting the trip. He already has the permission of Mustapha Mond, so the Director cannot object. But the Director does reminisce about his own experience at the Savage Reservation years ago and how he left a girl there. Bernard and Lenina make the trip and prepare at Santa Fé for the next jump. The Warden signs their permit, but before they enter the Reservation, Bernard discovers in a telephone conversation with Helmholtz that the Director plans to have him sent to Iceland. Even so, Lenina convinces Bernard to take soma and they fly to Malpais.

Ascending the mesa is difficult, and for Lenina the life of the Indians seems strange and offensive. Bernard and Lenina witness a corn ritual with a flogging. When it is over they meet a boy named John, who is evidently not Indian but who lives among the people. He takes them to meet his mother, who turns out to be Linda, the woman whom the Director left in the Reservation years before. To her shame, she bore John by natural means, and now she is fat and ugly, living a sordid life as an outsider with an outcast lover. While she tells Lenina about her life, John tells Bernard enough to make him realize the full story of his origins. Bernard formulates a plan and gets permission directly from Mustapha Mond to bring Linda and John back when he returns.

The Director has prepared a public humiliation of Bernard Marx for his subversive and antisocial behaviour. He plans to banish him to Iceland in disgrace. Instead, Marx introduces Linda and John to the assembled crowd. Their words and the Director's reactions prove the Director's guilt, and he rushes out, never to return to his post. Now Bernard Marx basks in the notoriety of the Savage whose care he has been given. And he changes from society's outcast to a popular figure who indulges in every aspect of the society. His head is so swelled by his new fame that he forgets himself in his reports to Mustapha Mond, who bides his time to strike at this impudent man.

The Savage becomes increasingly disillusioned with the new world which his mother recalled with such delight. Linda meanwhile takes increasing doses of soma and slowly dies, although she is unaware of the process. The Savage has always liked Lenina, and he goes with her to the feely, *Three Weeks in a Helicopter*. Although she is aroused by the feely, he is repulsed. He still considers her to be a sweet virginal girl. He thinks of her in the romantic terms Shakespeare used for his most chaste heroines. Finally, when Lenina tries to force a relationship directly, the Savage lashes out at her in a fury, threatening to kill her. Just after this threat the Savage is called to see his mother.

Having rejected the new world's technological wonders, the Savage visits his dying mother in the Hospital for the Dying. She is having a soma experience, and when he startles her into reality, she dies. In grief over her death, the Savage encounters a scene of Deltas about to receive their soma from a bursar. He hurls the soma in handfuls out a window while proclaiming the Deltas' freedom from the poisoning drug. The Deltas become a mob, ready to tear him apart. Fortunately the police arrive and break up the mob, but not before Helmholtz and Bernard have arrived to assist the Savage. The three friends are taken to see Mustapha Mond.

The World Controller speaks mainly to the Savage. In the course of the talk, Bernard breaks down and has to be taken into another room to be tranquillized. Mond gives Helmholtz a choice of islands to which to be exiled, and Helmholtz chooses the Falkland Islands. Finally, when Helmholtz has gone to see if Bernard is all right, Mond and the Savage discuss a subject not broached before in the novel — God. Mond, who knows Shakespeare, reveals the Bible and other theological works. Although he claims that God is known now only by an absence, the Savage disagrees. The Savage chooses to live with pain in solitude.

The Savage tries to make a life for himself in a lighthouse in Surrey, but he is discovered there and before long is plagued with visitors from the press and one feely-maker. Now he is not a recluse, but a celebrity. A horde of visitors rushes on him after the release of a film taken of him in one of his frenzied self-flagellations. The crowd calls for the whip, and the Savage produces it. Then Lenina appears, and the Savage has a focus for his frustration and rage. He beats her and then himself, but then the crowd joins in, in an orgy of beating. The next day when the Savage awakens, he is ashamed. When more curiosity seekers come that day, he is found hanging under the beams of the lighthouse.

Characters in the Novel

Arch-Community Songster of Canterbury: The ranking guest at one of Bernard Marx's parties given in honour of the Savage. Because of the Savage's non-appearance, the Arch-Community Songster leaves abruptly with Lenina, later to "have" her and give her a Fordian "T."

Assistant Director of Predestination: A friend of Henry Foster, the first to mention the exciting new feely, *Three Weeks in a Helicopter.*

Darwin Bonaparte: The famous wild-game feely-maker whose feely *The Savage of Surrey*, made live at the lighthouse hermitage of John the Savage, captures the imagination of the western world and sends hordes of curiosity seekers to see the freak in his habitat.

Fanny Crowne: Friend of Lenina Crowne and typical female in the new world order, versed in all the maxims of her sleep-teaching, yet ordered by Dr. Wells, her physician, to take Pregnancy Substitute medicine on account of the way she has been feeling.

Lenina Crowne: The most desirable woman in the novel, having "had" nearly everyone. She goes to the Savage Reservation with Bernard Marx, and develops an odd attraction to John, the Savage.

Director of Hatcheries and Conditioning: The pompous superior of Bernard Marx, to whom he makes a confession about having left a young girl at the Savage Reservation, thus paving the way for his own downfall, since Marx brings the girl Linda and his son John, the Savage, face to face with him just when he plans to denounce Marx. The director is called Tomakin by Linda.

Henry Ford: The great American industrialist, inventor of the conveyor-driven production line and maker of the Model T Ford, now revered as a deity since nearly all aspects of this futuristic society stem from his ideas; even the calendar indicates the years as After Ford (A.F.)

Henry Foster: Technician at the Central London Hatchery and Conditioning Centre who often dates Lenina Crowne and even recommends her heartily to his friends; a competent man who enjoys the usual pleasures of his culture — plenty of women, plenty of *soma*, and plenty of activities, such as Obstacle Golf.

Dr. Gaffney: The Provost of Eton who gives John, the Savage, a tour of his school and tells him that he thinks the film of *Penitentes* whipping themselves in religious frenzy is funny.

Benito Hoover: A goodnatured, even overly friendly man who would like to take Lenina Crowne to the North Pole for a vacation.

John, the Savage: Natural child (in the new world his birth would be considered unnatural) of the Director of Hatcheries and Conditioning and Linda, born on the Savage Reservation and raised under the most squalid conditions. Taken to London by Bernard Marx, he is disgusted by what he finds there, and so attempts to make a life of solitude for himself in Surrey, where he is found, hounded, and eventually commits suicide. John, the Savage is attracted to Lenina Crowne, whom he at first regards as a pure and virginal girl but whom he grows to hate because of her new-world sensuality.

Miss Keate: The Head Mistress at Eton, for whom Bernard Marx feels an attraction so strong that he must demonstrate it while they watch the film of the *Penitentes* whipping themselves.

Kiakimé: The young Indian girl whom John, the Savage loved, but who married Kothlu, an Indian boy, instead.

Linda: The unlucky date of the Director of Hatcheries and Conditioning, who was left at the Savage Reservation, bore a son, John, and became a degenerate, whore and drunkard. Upon returning to her own world, Linda overdoses with *soma* and dies with her son by her side.

Bernard Marx: The deformed Alpha-Plus who is the chief new-world character in the novel; a misfit and malcontent until he gains respect through his association with the Savage. Bernard is happy to embrace society until he is once again an outcast and finally is exiled to the Falkland Islands with his friend Helmholtz Watson.

Primo Mellon: The reporter for *The Hourly Radio* who tries to interview John, the Savage, at his retreat in Surrey but who receives only a savage kick, the report of which begins the Savage's seige of unwanted guests.

Old Mitsima: The old Indian at Malpais who teaches John, the Savage all about Indian lore, customs and survival; a kindly father figure for John and one of the finest people in all of Huxley's writings.

Mustapha Mond: Resident World Controller for Western Europe, one of the most powerful people in the new world, literally controlling society, though pleased that he has power to censor, punish, break laws, read forbidden books, and the like. He seems to enjoy talking to students about history and to the Savage about religion.

Palowhtiwa: Victim in the sacrificial rite on the mesa witnessed by Bernard Marx and Lenina Crowne; John, the Savage being jealous of his role as victim.

Popé: A degenerate in the Indian community who becomes Linda's pimp and lover, bringing her *mescal* and providing her with a sordid home life; John, the Savage, resenting what Popé does to Linda, hates him and tries unsuccessfully to kill him with a knife.

Reuben Rabinovitch: Small boy whose ability to repeat a lecture he heard while asleep stimulates the whole study of hypnopaedia, or sleep-teaching.

Morgana Rothschild: Woman with one enormous black eyebrow who sits next to Bernard Marx at a Solidarity Service at the Fordson Community Singery; Marx cannot get her hideous eyebrow out of his mind and fails to achieve a sense of mystic attainment in the service (other members of the service include Fifi Bradlaugh, Jim Bokanovsky, Clara Deterding, the President of the Group, Joanna Diesel, Sarojini Engels, Herbert Bakunin, and Tom Kawaguchi).

William Shakespeare: Greatest writer of all time in the English language, whose works are found by Popé in the chests of the Antelope Kiva and form the basis of the education and world view of John, the Savage.

Dr. Shaw: Physician attending the dying Linda; he is thankful to have such an unusual specimen of senility to study.

Warden of the Reservation: Garrulous keeper of the Savage Reservation who enjoys trying to scare Lenina with statistics and descriptions of what lies inside, with little success.

Helmholtz Watson: Friend of Bernard Marx and also later of the Savage, a superior Alpha-Plus with a facility at emotional engineering that is unparalleled; broods that good writing is impossible in the new world and becomes interested in Shakespeare — to a point; is exiled to the Falkland Islands for supporting the Savage in the incident at the Hospital for the Dying.

Chapter by Chapter
Summaries and Commentaries

CHAPTER 1

Summary

The Director of the Central London Hatchery and Conditioning Centre ushers a group of male students through the Fertilizing Room, with its sterile, white atmosphere and its 300 mechanical workers intent on their instruments. The year is After Ford (A.F.) 632. As the Director points out details of the fertilization procedure, ingrained sayings emerge as if from the collective mind of the new culture: "generalities are intellectually necessary evils" or "rams wrapped in thermogene beget no lambs."

Voluntary operations on selected females yield ovaries from which eggs are taken, then fertilized and processed as Alphas, Betas, Gammas, Deltas, or Epsilons, the latter three being created in multitudes by Bokanovsky's process, which causes eggs to divide and proliferate. Thus thousands of "twins" identical in most respects can be produced from a single budding egg, by forcing it to divide.

As the students mindlessly record every word of the Director's speech, they witness the mechanical processes that ensure uniformity and "social stability." One ovary can yield 15,000 adult individuals. Mr. Foster, a zealous manager at the Centre, boasts of one ovary which produced 16,012 adults and asserts that they intend to beat the records of production set in Singapore and Mombasa.

Mr. Foster continues on the tour with facts and figures about the Bottling Room, where the embryos are stored and labelled for shipping to the Social Predestination Room and finally to the Embryo Store. Mr. Foster and the Director give details about how the Predestinators and Fertilizers interact.

In the basement, which is bathed in dim red light, the students witness the methods science prescribes for "gestation" and for sexual screening. Approximately seventy per cent of the females are dosed with male sex-hormone to render them sterile; they are then called "freemartins." Most gratifying to Mr. Foster is the social conditioning that separates out, once and for all, sewage workers from Directors of Hatcheries.

A Beta-Minus mechanic reduces the revolutions per minute so that less oxygen can get to certain embryos — those destined purposely to be stunted into Epsilons, the lowest social class. The Director and Mr. Foster consider how socially beneficial it would be to lower the age of maturity of Epsilons from eighteen to, say, ten years, so that eight additional years of useful work might be obtained from these unintelligent beings. Experimentation in this field of early maturation is far from complete.

The students see the Heat Conditioning tunnels, where embryos that will become tropical workers are given stimuli to condition them to enjoy a hot climate. Lenina, a nurse, is inoculating these embryos with typhoid and sleeping sickness, to prepare them for the tropics. Clearly there is more than a merely professional relationship between Lenina and Foster.

Foster describes the conditioning given to rocket-plane engineers, whose embryos are kept in constant motion, but he is cut off before he can show the students the Alpha-Plus Intellectuals. The Director allows one glance at the Decanting Room before herding the students to the Nurseries.

Commentary

Huxley's means of delivering his readers to the Brave New World is through the Central London Hatchery and Conditioning Centre. Clearly this one place has the flavour of what society has become in the age of biological assembly lines. The sterility of the building and the mechanical process that has supplanted normal human reproduction are symbols of the larger control that society has over the destinies of human beings. The motto of the World State — Community, Identity, Stability — obliterates ideas of individualism, freedom, and benign eccentricity.

Through this imagery of inhuman treatment of human life forms, Huxley suggests the wholly-transformed world order. Clearly the World State has supplanted other governments worldwide. Clearly the London Hatchery is just one of multitudes — Singapore and Mombasa being two others. In the tones of the Director and Foster, buoyant assurance is meant to override any doubt that society could be handled otherwise than it is. The citizens of this society are controlled from the very beginning, even before the creation of the egg in the extracted ovary. Society is clinically arranged, carefully conditioned to enjoy what it must endure.

The intellectual order is of primary importance in the Brave New World. At the top are the Alphas, and at the bottom are the Epsilons. At each level, only certain occupations are appropriate. Within each category there are Pluses and Minuses. From the moment of the melding of sperm and egg, the life conditioning begins. The heat conditioning for tropical workers and the motion conditioning for rocket engineers are typical of the kinds of treatments available over the complete range of beings.

The practical politics of the Brave New World are demonstrated in the interaction of the Director and Foster with each other and with the students. They work together like well-oiled machinery, often alternating lines of speech as if reading from a script. They flatter each other, the Director praising Foster's ambition and spirit (as well as his choice in women) and Foster insinuating that the Director is the foremost member of society. Their smugness leaves no room for opposition. When one student asks about the merit of Bokanovsky's Process, he is berated as if he were an idiot and given the unsatisfactory answer that the process is one of the major instruments of social stability. This is not a society where free inquiry is invited. The acceptable areas of investigation are in discovering how to increase the output of eggs from a single ovary, and how to lower the age of maturity of Epsilon morons. The students, the cream of the youth of this new society, are shown as servile, cowed, and unimaginative — wholly conditioned by their society. This one tour is the most general view the students will have of their subject, yet aside from the images of the bottles and spaces, all they will carry away is numbers and a few smug platitudes.

The Director is a pompous and powerful figure, the embodiment of the rules of his orderly society. Henry Foster is a man in love with numbers and analytical processes.

Colour is used symbolically throughout the book, and although fairly subtle in this first chapter, is poignant too. In the sterile whiteness of the laboratory, the living forms seen through the microscopes offer the only sympathetic note. Down in the cavernous, dark basement, the red light and the red splotches representing embryos stand in contrast to the mechanical conditioning and stifling methods used on the life forms. The students themselves are "pink and callow" at the start, as if they too are part of the life that is being managed very carefully by forces larger than themselves. They are in stark contrast to the "three red ghosts" unloading the demijohns in the basement. More sinister is the black question mark on the white ground that serves to mark the "freemartins," or sterilized females.

The use of the symbol of the biological assembly line is in keeping with the way this new society records its years from the time of Ford. Ford, of course, is the American industrialist Henry Ford (1863-1947), developer of the assembly line in American automobile production. His ideas revolutionized industry, and his automobiles revolutionized American life. Ford's concept of factory process was to simplify each task so that any man could master it, then align the workers so that the individual tasks could be accomplished in their proper order in the most efficient manner. Huxley has taken Ford's assembly line as the starting point for all later technology and as the symbol of the dehumanization of society as a whole. Ford was still alive when Huxley wrote *Brave New World*, and his conveyor-belt assembly line, by 1927, (four years before Huxley's conception of his novel) had produced more than 15 million Model T's. Huxley saw the process as a metaphor that, improperly applied, could transform society into a totalitarian monster.

CHAPTER 2

Summary
The Director leads the students into the Infant Nurseries on the fifth floor. There, nurses set out bowls of roses in a long row across the well-lit room. Then on the Director's order, they set out the books, opened to pictures of gaily-coloured birds or beasts. These being ready, the children, eight-month-old Deltas in khaki clothing, are deposited on the floor and turned towards the flowers and books. As the children arrive at the row of flowers and begin to take delight in touching and crumpling the flowers and books, the Director signals the Head Nurse to press a lever. An explosion, a shrill siren, alarm bells, and, at the pressing of a second lever, an electric shock, terrify the babies. Then, after the stimuli are removed, the babies are once again shown the flowers and books, but this time they shriek in horror. The Director is delighted with this exercise since, repeated, it will lead to an instinctive hatred of books and flowers.

One student, though understanding why society could not have Deltas wasting time with books, asks about the flowers.

The Director explains that the masses must be conditioned to hate the country but to love country sports, for which they consume material goods and use transportation systems.

The Director tells the tale of Reuben Rabinovitch. In the process he must give some unpleasant background — about a dead language called Polish and about parents, which are no longer necessary in society. Young Reuben heard a radio broadcast of a talk by George Bernard Shaw. The boy was asleep at the time, but the next morning he was able to repeat the broadcast. This was the beginning of the principle of sleep-teaching, or "hypnopaedia." Even though this case occurred only 23 years after Our Ford's first Model T, an effective method of using the technique was developed much later. This was because the early attempts were to implant information. Only later was hypnopaedia used for moral education, which, the Director maintains, ought never be rational.

The group proceeds to the fourteenth floor and is warned to be silent on arrival. There, in a dormitory, are eighty cots in a row against a wall, each containing a boy or girl Beta. Each is being taught by a recording. The recording is indoctrination in Elementary Class Consciousness. Wordless training, such as the Delta's electric shocks, is not sufficient. The repetition of the words that reinforce class consciousness make the mind one coherent conviction. The Director becomes so wrapped up in his explanations that he bangs on a table as he revels in the triumph of the method, and wakes the children.

Commentary

The first chapter showed the biological controls that could be imposed on the embryos of the future adults of the Brave New World. The second chapter is an introduction to the way this society treats its infants and children. The controls now are of two distinct kinds. First there is direct stimulation — negatives like the shocks and sirens to discourage the young Deltas from liking flowers and books. But these wordless methods do not give the children the refined class distinctions that the hypnopaedia techniques do. In both cases — the shocks and the verbal repetitions — reinforcement is essential. As with the experiments of the Russian scientist, Pavlov, the changes must be deep — so deep that responses seem natural.

The nurseries are called Neo-Pavlovian Conditioning Rooms. Pavlov's inhumane treatment of animals to discover their instincts caused great fear, lest his techniques should be tried out on humans. In Brave New World technology, Pavlov's techniques have been incorporated with others to control society at a deep psychological level. A conditioned response infallibly keeps society running smoothly.

The story of Reuben Rabinovitch suggests much more than hypnopaedia. When Huxley wrote *Brave New World*, in 1931, twenty-three years after the first Model T was put on the market, he was using the latest discoveries and extending them to the limits of the human imagination. George Bernard Shaw was a moralist, individualist, and iconoclast. It is ironical that his lecture on his own genius should provide the material for the later enslavement of mankind.

Unlike Rabinovitch, the Alpha students who are listening to the Director have no parents, in our understanding of the word. In fact, the very words "mother" and "father" are obscenities to them. Old-fashioned parental control, always imperfect, has been supplanted by state control. Now, no young Rabinovitch happens to hear a radio broadcast unless it is intended that he should. In fact, the very name Rabinovitch, with its clearly Jewish origins, would have no place in the new order.

Tommy, the boy subjected to the "wrong" kind of hypnopaedia, could only repeat his whole lesson verbatim. He did not understand it at all. The Director explains that moral education is somehow different from informational education.

Notice that the two forms of "moral" education given to the young Betas are Elementary Sex and Elementary Class Consciousness. Although no indication is given in this chapter as to what sex education means, it clearly has nothing to do with parents, courtship, or child-rearing. Class consciousness is clearly delineated. The Beta is to distinguish himself or herself from the lower forms — Gammas, who are stupid and wear green, Deltas who are worse and wear khaki, and Epsilons who are still worse and who wear black. Lack of intelligence (so-called) is the main reason for the separation of classes, and classes are colour-coded so that there can be no mistake in identification. The Betas are made to feel no pressure to become Alphas, because Alphas work too hard. Besides they wear grey.

Although labelled "elementary," this kind of education gives the irreducible categories into which human beings may be placed.

Huxley uses the metaphor of sealing wax for the process. The whole of the consciousness is covered over, as if with one continuous red mass. This is an echo of the image of the red blob of the embryonic stage. The mind and memory are as controlled as the foetus was in the early stages of life. And with the mind, the fate of each person is sealed. What such a mind can suggest has been programmed for it to suggest. It is part of the larger continuous mind of the state.

The Director's lapse from self-control (though he is an Alpha, conditioned like all the rest) is just one of many indications planted in the novel that this so-called perfect state cannot suppress human emotions. The unplanned appearance of the sunshine in the Deltas' nursery is another indication that the world is full of surprises that may work for or against the designs of the controllers. For now these are just hints.

The nurses in this chapter are shadowy figures. Much more important are the figures of Reuben and Tommy, who stand out as real and palpable against a backdrop of less vital throngs of electrified Deltas and sleep-conditioned Betas. These two boys suggest more about the limits and possibilities of human beings than do the hosts of controlled beings in the Brave New World.

CHAPTER 3

Summary

The Director and his students observe six or seven hundred naked children in the garden, playing games such as Centrifugal Bumble-puppy, designed to increase consumption. Some children are playing rudimentary sexual games. A nurse drags away a young boy who abnormally will not submit to sexual play. The Director tells his little-girl partner, whose name is Polly Trotsky, to find herself another little boy.

The Director tells the students something of the history of erotic play among children. Before Ford and even afterwards, erotic play was considered abnormal — even immoral, up to the age of twenty years! The students ask the results, and a new voice tells them the results were terrible. The new voice belongs to Mustapha Mond, the Controller, whom the Director identifies for his students.

(With this identification, the narrative begins to become fragmented, many strands separating until they are no more than single lines of speech. This is Huxley's way of implying the wholeness of the fabric he has woven together. For simplicity, the various strands are separated below.)

Mustapha Mond: The students are most impressed by the surprise intrusion of the Resident Controller for Western Europe, one of ten controllers of the whole world. He begins with Ford's famous statement that history is bunk. Although the Director is uncomfortable about his doing so, the Controller proceeds to give the students some background — what it meant to have had a mother and live with a family, what a home was. His evocation of what a home was makes some students sick. He purposefully blends the name Ford with that of the psychologist, Freud, and he contrasts an ancient world of strife and self-direction with the present situation in which "everyone belongs to everyone else." With the triad of mother, monogamy, and romance, humankind was under enormous pressure, and release meant instability. Yet social stability is essential, and the whole of society must be tended by sane men tending the sanely-turning wheels. With a wave of the hand, Mond indicates stability in the world around him. He says that infinite pains have been taken to make the students' lives emotionally easy. He challenges them to tell him of an instance of their having to encounter an insurmountable obstacle. One of the boys tells of a four-week interval in which a girl he wanted would not let him have her.

Mond goes on to give some background to the establishment of the new order. Ectogenesis had to wait. Sleep-teaching had to wait. Division by class had to wait. There was the Nine Years' War in A.F. 141. In all the horrors of war, there was a choice between World Control and destruction. At first force was attempted, but finally a combination of ectogenesis, neo-Pavlovian conditioning, and hypnopaedia prevailed. There followed the destruction of historical repositories and the banning of books published before A.F. 150. The pyramids, Shakespeare, God, all disappeared. Crosses were lopped off to form the sacred "T" of Ford. To supplant pain killers like alcohol, morphia, and cocaine, thousands of subsidized pharmacologists and biochemists developed the perfect drug — soma. Then through a combination of developments, the signs of old age were eradicated, and old men were forever spared the pain of thinking. The Controller tells his disciple-students to allow children to come to him.

The Centre: At four o'clock the main day-shift is called off duty and the second day-shift is called on. The conveyors continue relentlessly as Henry Foster, Bernard Marx, and Lenina Crowne, among others, proceed from work to pleasure. Throughout the ensuing interlaced dialogues and thoughts, the machinery continues, and the chapter ends with a reminder of those bottles revolving in the red-lighted darkness.

Bernard Marx: He is introduced in the elevator with Henry Foster (from Chapter 1) and his assistant. He is repulsed by the conversation between Henry and his assistant about a "Feely" that features love-making on a bearskin rug. Bernard is contemptuous as Foster speaks in the stale hypnopaedic formulas. Marx is a psychologist and specialist in hypnopaedia. He is also an Alpha-Plus, though somewhat smaller than his class. Foster and the assistant agree that he looks unnaturally glum, and they bait him with advice that he take soma. They are successful since he not only refuses but rails at them. They laugh at him, and he grumbles as he walks down the corridor.

Lenina Crowne: She is the one who has received the three pats from the Director in Chapter 1, and now her mind is split between thoughts about her present lover, Henry Foster, and this strange Bernard Marx. In the Girls' Dressing Room, she meets her friend Fanny who works in the Bottling Room. Fanny's name is also Crowne. Lenina bathes, powders herself, and vibro-vacs herself. She returns to discover that her friend Fanny is planning not to go out tonight but instead to take a Pregnancy Substitute. It is clear from the medicines in her locker that female systems medicine is not easy in the Brave New World. Fanny will have to refrain from going with men for about a week.

Lenina is still going with Henry Foster after four months and has to defend herself to Fanny, who says the Director would be furious if he knew she had no one else all that time. Foster himself has had others during the time, and the Director himself is normal — witness his pats. Lenina has not been feeling promiscuous, and Fanny admits that she has been in the same state, but they agree she should make the effort to be more outgoing. At this point Lenina mentions Bernard Marx's invitation to the Savage Reservation. Fanny is horrified because of Marx's reputation. Not only does he avoid playing Obstacle Golf, he likes to be alone.

Fanny objects that Marx is ugly and short. She brings up the rumour that Marx's embryo bottle was contaminated with alcohol so that his growth was stunted. But Lenina insists that she will accept his invitation, and she tries to deflect criticism on the grounds that she wants to see the Savage Reservation.

Lenina and Fanny dress back to back in silence, and when they are dressed Lenina tries to mend fence. Lenina is dressed stunningly in green with a contraceptive belt, and Fanny cannot help but admire it. She asks Lenina to ask Foster where he got the Malthusian belt so that she can get one too.

Meanwhile, to Bernard Marx's annoyance, Foster and the assistant have compared Lenina and Fanny minutely as to their sexual abilities, Foster recommending to the assistant that he try Lenina as soon as possible.

Commentary

After having set the stage by providing a glimpse of the methods of controlling life and thought patterns from birth through early childhood in the Brave New World, Huxley now thrusts forward simultaneously the full historical background *and* a human situation that is very complex. Mustapha Mond, one of the ten World Controllers, is at the very top of this society, and he appropriately tells just how the present world came to be formed. As he develops this in fragmentary form, the human drama is established in the interaction of three men and two women. Mond declares that human misery is now at an end because of the new order. But for Marx, the new order is not Paradise. Like the small boy who was taken from the garden for not wishing to perform sexual acts, Marx is repulsed by the animality implied by the attitudes of his companions in the elevator. Marx is an Alpha-Plus, a member of the top intellectual class, yet he is deformed in shape and attitudes.

Huxley is wise not to belabour the details of the imposition of the new order. In the fragments of Mond's account, the Nine Years' War and the triumph of the methods of societal control are all that seem necessary. His tale is one of victory over human misery by means of total societal control. And he is talking to the cream of the crop — Alphas. Mond relates the industrial and psychological revolutions that formed the new order in the confusion, or fusion, of the names Ford and Freud. Sigmund Freud, the initiator of depth psychology, even more than Pavlov, provides the basis for the sexual emphasis in the new order. And it is no accident that the emerging protagonist in this part of the novel is himself a psychologist, quite aware of the tricks used to shape the consciousness of his contemporaries.

Huxley develops his human story by means of stark contrasts. The two men, Foster and Marx, are opposites. Both like Lenina, but their approaches are different. Foster is "normal" in his appreciation of her superior sexual abilities; Marx is "abnormal" in his veneration of her. Likewise the two women are opposites. Lenina has become too attached to Foster, where Fanny has become ill and needs a Pregnancy Substitute. Lenina has responded to Marx's strange veneration of her, where Fanny is repulsed by Marx's outward strangeness. The attraction of one woman — Lenina — for two men — Foster and Marx, is complicated by the apparent unconcern of Foster that she be possessed by someone else and by the desperate concern of Marx that she be something other than what she is.

Two new ideas are presented but not developed fully in this chapter — *soma* and the Savage Reservation. *Soma*, the drug that supplanted all other means to make people happy, is alluded to by Mond, Foster and his assistant, the two women, and (by negative reaction) Marx. It is so much a part of the environment that it is essential. Without soma this new order would be inconceivable. It is the only agent that always banishes care. Marx is the only one who refuses to accept its power. Almost equivalent to *soma* is the Savage Reservation. It, too, seems to be an answer to the new order. Yet at this point in the story it is only an exotic place. Marx is associated with it only in his invitation to take Lenina there. Since the whole world is unified through its values and since Marx is aware of the world insofar as the highest intellectual order can be, the Savage Reservation must be connected with Marx's strangeness. He both rejects *soma* and is attracted to the Reservation.

Bernard Marx is so far the most interesting character presented. He is a rebel. He does not seem to fit into the perfect society presented in the first pages. Although a story about his being spoiled in the test tube seems to account for his physical size and appearance, it is never substantiated by facts. The name

Marx may well come from the name Karl Marx, and the name Bernard might well come from George Bernard Shaw, but there are many other possibilities. This character is naturally easier to accept for a modern reader than, say, Foster, because he is more thoughtful, more critical of societal norms, and more reverent towards women. He is also sympathetic because deformed, yet well regarded because he is intelligent and a psychologist.

Sexuality is a major focus at this point in the book. The problem of the generation of the species being left in the laboratory, Huxley now explores human relations in a world without traditional taboos. And he has purposely set out to see just how far he can go. Children at play practise sex. Adults are expected to perform regularly and with many persons of the opposite sex. Refraining is a kind of sin, as practising sex seemed to be a kind of sin before the new order. Coupling too often with the same person is suspect, and chemical and biological safeguards are available if weakness is suspected. Everyone belongs to everyone else. Monogamy, like motherhood, is antisocial. So new taboos are erected in place of the old ones.

CHAPTER 4

Summary
In the lift Lenina notices Bernard Marx and says she will be glad to go to New Mexico with him in July. She cannot understand why Bernard should feel embarrassed about her mentioning this trip, even though the lift is crowded with other men who have had her before. On the roof the two exchange a few words, and she reminds him to let her know about the trip beforehand, as she flits off to meet Foster. Benito Hoover says a few good-natured things and reaches for some *soma* to share with Marx, but Marx hurries off.

Henry Foster and Lenina take off in his helicopter. They observe the countryside and suburbs of London alive with people of different classes, seeking the sports that fit them best. Finally they land at Stoke Poges and play Obstacle Golf.

(Part 2)
Sensitive to the remarks of Benito Hoover, who had meant no harm, and to the casual way Lenina had made him suffer, Bernard Marx sharply orders two Delta-Minus attendants to

ready his machine. Marx feels the inferiority of a man who does not measure up to his class physically, and he envies Henry Foster and Benito Hoover who have the size and looks to be respected by the lower classes.

Finally in flight, Bernard Marx heads for the roof of the Propaganda House and, arriving there, he has a Gamma-Plus porter announce his presence to Helmholtz Watson, Alpha-Plus lecturer at the College of Emotional Engineering and a working Emotional Engineer. Where Marx has a physical defect, Helmholtz has an intellectual excess. The men share the knowledge that they are individuals. Helmholtz does everything well and is a universal champion, but at bottom is searching for something else — and Bernard assists him in discovering what that might be. Helmholtz eludes three enticing women and makes the waiting plane to tell Marx that he has been cutting committees and girls, and Marx tells Helmholtz that he has asked Lenina to go to New Mexico with him. The two men go to Marx's room, where they stretch out on sofas and talk.

Helmholtz complains that he has the power to make a statement and feels compelled to make it, but that he does not know what the statement is. He feels he ought to say something important, more than just another catchy saying that depends on the network of known hypnopaedic sayings. He feels he writes about nothing. In response Marx says he thinks someone is at the door. When Helmholtz has verified that no one is there, Marx gives himself up to self-pity, making Helmholtz feel somewhat ashamed for him.

Commentary

Bernard is the one character who unifies this chapter, and his inadequacies not only make us question his role as the novel's hero, but also the place of heroism in this new society. His stature causes him a sense of inferiority, but when he cringes under the social pressures caused by Lenina's statement in the lift or when he purposefully stops his friend's conversation so as to divert the focus to his own self-pity, he shrinks beneath contempt.

Henry Foster's assurance in handling his helicopter and his exactitude in every detail of his world make him capable, but there is nothing heroic about him. He is merely competent. He has no nobility of soul. He is not capable of suffering. He has or can obtain everything he might want. Just as Lenina's conversation seems bound to repeat the lessons of hypnopaedia, so Foster's seems to revolve around whether people and rockets are on schedule — or by how much they are not on schedule.

Helmholtz seems at first to be better material than Foster. He not only has what he wants — he has much more than any other man can handle. Not just one, but three women want to monopolize him on an Exmoor picnic. He sets records with women and with committees, but somehow being heroic in this way satisfies neither him nor us. He is the best Alpha-Plus offered, better by far than Bernard Marx, but he has only a vague sense that he must make a statement. He is so close to the pulse-beat of his community that he can dash off slogans by the minute. His ramblings in his talks with Marx show that he is searching for something else. He has given up girls and committees to intensify his search. Yet his sacrifices seem trivial. And when he gets close to a real truth about his society — that it is, after all, "nothing," and "Can you say something about nothing?" he is cut off mindlessly by his only friend.

Helmholtz's abilities do not seem rooted in any reservoir of deep passion. On the other hand, Bernard Marx does not seem able to remove himself from his consideration of the human condition. The two friends together show the impossibility of heroism in the new order. Both are misfits, and because they are, they are individuals. Yet neither is admirable. Helmholtz has mastered the society's rhetoric as if it were an elaborate game. Marx has the sensitivity to recognize the hollow ring of the society's formulas. Helmholtz is looking for another possibility because he is in tune with society; Marx is dissatisfied because he is out of tune with it.

The two leisure-time activities shown here are Obstacle Golf and confessional conversation. Underlying the human interaction in each case is an inability to communicate at all levels. The conversation of Foster and Lenina, no less than that of Helmholtz and Bernard, is superficial. Whether they know it or not, the supposedly unified people in the new order are isolated and made to feel guilty for it, by propaganda.

Huxley's satire in this chapter involves the depth-level commentary on heroism and the human condition, but it also involves the great fun of remaking the London suburbs into a futuristic pleasure garden, overrun with uniformed people, congregating by kind, and of swelling to monstrous size the buildings and public works enterprises. The futuristic Fleet Street, pictured as a giant propaganda centre, alludes as much to the present-day abuses of the media as the future ones. The comedy is tinged with irony in each case.

CHAPTER 5

Summary

At eight o'clock Lenina and Henry leave their game and take off into the evening, where from a height they can observe the landscape and buildings. They view the Internal and External Secretions factory and the Slough Crematorium. The stacks of the Crematorium, Henry explains, have devices for phosphorus recovery, making even a person's death a socially useful event. The couple discuss the chemical equality of men, as well as the social usefulness of everyone. As they fly over the Crematorium, they swoop upwards in a jet of hot air, which is a person disappearing forever. The two console themselves that everyone is happy now.

They dine at Henry's apartment house, take *soma*, and retreat to the Westminster Abbey Cabaret, where they hear their favourite song and dance with hundreds of others. After more *soma* the two move back to Henry's rooms and, after she takes her contraceptive precautions, Lenina asks where he bought the cartridge belt so that she can tell Fanny later.

(Part 2)

Bernard dines at the Aphroditaeum with Helmholtz, then takes a taxi to the Fordson Community Singery for his Solidarity Group meeting. He is delighted to see that he is not the last to arrive — three of the twelve seats around the circular table are still empty. Unluckily, he sits next to Morgana Rothschild. Finally the table is full, man-woman-man in a circle, and the ceremony begins. *Soma* is passed around and hymns are sung. At the end of the second hymn the *soma* has begun to work, and after the third everyone seems to have a sense of the Coming. After a number of the others have jumped up to testify to the Coming, Bernard does so, though he really has felt nothing. He dances with the rest in their ritual and sings "Orgy-porgy." He collapses with the rest on one of a ring of couches.

Afterwards Fifi asks Bernard whether the event was not wonderful. Bernard lies and says it was. Now he feels more alone than ever, having witnessed the others achieve the sense of oneness that he could not achieve.

Commentary

Two kinds of ritual are satirized in this chapter. The first is the ritual of dating in the new world. The golfing is followed by dinner with *soma*, dancing at a cabaret, and sleeping with the date. The second is a more elevated ritual in some respects. It is the almost-religious society meeting with its orgiastic overtones and its commingling of souls into a greater spirit. *Soma* is the potent agent in each case for achieving a state above normality. The events portrayed are, by implication, occurring throughout the society. These events are not isolated, but communal.

Henry and Lenina dance among hundreds to the music of Sexophonists; Bernard, Morgana and the rest, twelve in all, dance to music engineered by the President of their society. "Bottle of Mine" expresses the wish never to have left the comfort of the womb-like bottled state. "Orgy-porgy" in contrast speaks of a release through sexual contact that never comes. While the couple ends the evening in bed, in physical contact, the twelve end it having presumably had a feeling of oneness exhausted around the meeting room.

Rather than being fulfilled by the experience of Solidarity, Bernard feels more alone and dissatisfied than ever. Morgana Rothschild's continuous eyebrow seems to symbolize Bernard's incapacity to meld with the group or with the supposed spiritual presence the others say they feel.

The Cabaret's atmosphere is meant to be a parody of the cabarets of Huxley's time. The Solidarity Service is more difficult to explain. It is a blend of a social club ritual and a religious revival service. The drugs, hymns, testimonials, body movements, and rhythmic dancing seem pagan in origin, though the sign of the T and other details are reminiscent of a Christian ritual. The strawberry ice-cream *soma* is a parody of the Christian Communion, and the Coming a parody of the presence of God. Again Huxley has used events that are similar enough to allow a connection across broad swaths of society. Whether in the masses or in the elite, a kind of mindless pleasure-seeking is the norm, and *soma* is the primary sign of pleasure.

Bernard does not seem susceptible to the group hysteria, but Lenina's prosaic question about the origin of her belt brings into question all the releases of this society. How much is self-deception? Is Bernard only incapable of playing the game? Lenina, as a result of indoctrination, has been trained to use contraceptives under any and all conditions. Even under the influence of *soma* she does not forget. Bernard's mind seems to have a natural contraceptive against melding with the crowd. He is unable to feel confident about the Coming. Even as the crowd dances in a red light exactly like that in the Embryo Store, even under the influence of *soma*, even with music pounding and with the motion of his own body, Bernard cannot surrender.

"Orgy-porgy" is a corruption of the nursery rhyme, "Georgie-Porgie," an unlikely jingle for a profound ritual. Bernard Marx seems oblivious of the ludicrousness of the ritual — he only blames himself for having his "dead satiety."

CHAPTER 6

Summary

Lenina begins to reconsider her decision to go to New Mexico with Bernard Marx. He is so odd, and yet very few people have ever visited the Savage Reservation. The alternative would be a boring trip to the North Pole with Benito Hoover.

Discussing Bernard with Henry Foster, Lenina discovers that Henry thinks Bernard is a harmless rhinoceros, who just does not respond to conditioning. Particularly disquieting for Lenina is Bernard's desire to do things in private. For Lenina, crowds and standard kinds of organized fun are safe; she cannot understand what Bernard enjoys about walking and just talking.

Lenina convinces Bernard that they should attend the Women's Heavyweight Wrestling Championship in Amsterdam. Bernard goes, but is glum and even rude. On the way back he stops their helicopter in mid-flight above the English Channel, close to the waves to watch a night storm. Linda is terrified not only of the storm but of Bernard's dangerous statements about wanting to be free. Although he feels that he and Lenina should be able to be more together alone above the waves, she thinks otherwise. So he abruptly takes her back to his rooms and gives her the time she expects, complete with radio, television, and *soma*.

The next afternoon Lenina looks for praise, which Bernard gives her, though secretly he knows she is just so much "meat." When he says he wishes the evening did not end in their going to bed, she is upset. Her discomfort increases as he explains his wish that instead of acting like children, people would act like adults all the time. All she can speak are the statements ingrained by sleep-teaching.

(Part 2)

Bernard visits the Director to have him initial the already-approved permit for his trip to the Savage Reservation. The Director surprises Bernard by reminiscing about a trip he once made to New Mexico when he was Bernard's age. He took a blonde Beta-Minus, who strayed away from him and was lost in the Reservation. The Director admits that he even dreams about the incident sometimes. When he realizes Bernard is giving him a critical eye, he defends himself first by denying that he had an indecorous relationship with the girl, then by turning against Marx's work performance and his lapses from "infantile decorum." Instead of being downcast by the warning, Bernard exults in the persecution. That evening he lies a bit about the interview to make Helmholtz admire him. But Helmholtz is ashamed for his friend's boasting and gloating.

(Part 3)

Bernard and Lenina arrive by the Blue Pacific Rocket in Santa Fé, and stay at a hotel with all the amenities of civilization. Bernard warns her that there are no such luxuries in the Reservation, yet she says she wants to go. The Warden of the Reservation admits them the next morning and drones on about the Reservation. He is a mine of irrelevant information. The situation is ludicrous because Bernard remembers he has left a cologne dispenser on in his bathroom, and wishes to escape to have it turned off. Lenina, on the other hand, has taken *soma* and made her mind blank even though she appears to be in rapt attention.

Some facts presented by the Warden are graphic: an electrified fence that kills surrounds the Reservation, where children are still born and suckled. There is no communication permitted with the outside world.

Bernard breaks free to have Helmholtz turn off the cologne

dispenser, only to discover that the Director has decided to replace him and send him to Iceland. While before, Bernard imagined himself eager for a great trial, now all courage leaves him. Interrupting his railing, Lenina gets him to take some *soma*, and, in another mood, they set off on a tour. After seeing the fence lined with bones of electrified creatures, Bernard falls asleep and awakens only when they have reached the rest-house. Before he leaves, their pilot assures them that the savages are harmless.

Commentary

Lenina's decision to stick with her plan to go to the Savage Reservation with Bernard Marx is not elaborated at great length by Huxley. Presumably Lenina is not a deep thinker. She is substituting an exotic, unknown place for an exotic, known place — the North Pole. Bernard is strange, but not so strange that she will change her plans, even after the experience over the English Channel. Lenina's tastes have not changed. She still wants to seek out crowds. And she sees no value in being alone with someone unless she is making love with him. Exactly why she goes — and why she does not stay at the comfortable hotel in Santa Fé — remains a mystery.

Bernard is revealed in each of the three parts of this chapter, but the revelations of his character offer no surprises. In the first part he is unhappy and tries to convey his unhappiness to a person who has no means of understanding him. In the second part he gains an opportunity that is very rare in his society, but he betrays just how conditioned he himself is by not responding sympathetically to the confession of the Director. This not only gives him the key to the Director's later downfall, but shows the dangers involved in betraying human feeling in the Brave New World. In the third part Bernard shows that he is not at the Reservation as a scholar. He is much too worried about running up a bill on cologne than listening to the Warden. And after he hears about the Director's moves against him, he is shown up as base and cowardly. He misses the sights on his tour because he falls asleep, the only image grasped beforehand being the deadly fence around the Reservation.

The scene with the Warden is well drawn, but it has a hidden purpose. On the surface the Warden's garrulity is a great bore, and his delay in signing the papers a source of comedy —

the couple are trapped until he does so. Yet the supposedly irrelevant information he gives them is the first real data the reader
has about this new place. The isolation of its inhabitants, the
electrified fence, the strange languages, customs, religious traditions, and peoples in this place delineate it as wholly different
from the Brave New World, more like our old world than the
new one. It is ironical that Bernard, seeing for the first time a
symbol of isolation of the elements that might make his dissatisfaction meaningful, is asleep, full of civilization's remedy —
soma.

The Director's lapse into memory and nostalgia is a major
social blunder. It is so bad, in his society's terms, that he must
seek to destroy the man who witnesses him in the alien state.
What triggers his mind is the phrase *New Mexican Reservation*.
And what triggers Bernard's response to him is the knowledge
that this memory is ignited in spite of the Director's opposition
to his going at all. And the story itself tells of an extraordinary
passion of a man for one woman. The recurrent dreams show
the power of the moment of loss. But the same power, shared by
Marx, directly threatens the Director. Huxley ironically uses the
anecdote, the most powerful in the book, to shape the rest of
the plot. The story itself is mythic, striking at the heart of a
tragic loss, and implying that such emotional depths are impossible even to relate, in the new world.

Where the Director unconsciously betrays himself, the
Warden has no luck at all in trying to shock the drugged Lenina,
and Bernard is too hopelessly delirious about his cologne to
react to the information given. Bernard's *soma* eliminates the
"roots and fruits" — the animosity of the Director and Bernard
and the new threat of Bernard's going to Iceland in exile — and
causes the "flower of the present" to blossom rosily. The
vegetable imagery used is appropriate, since the Indians that day
will be celebrating their summer festival.

CHAPTER 7

Summary
Lenina and Bernard are escorted by a smelly Indian guide
up onto the mesa that holds the pueblo of Malpais. As they
climb they hear the wild music, and on top they are met by half-
naked men in paint and feathers with snakes in their hands.

Lenina is horrified by nearly everything she witnesses — the dirt, the smell, the signs of old age in an ancient Indian who pauses to regard her. Unfortunately she and Bernard have forgotten their *soma*. Lenina is repulsed by two women openly suckling their young. Bernard rubs in the embarrassment, asking her to imagine doing the same.

Their guide leads them through a building to a terrace where they can hear sounds coming from the square below them, walled in except for a hole with a descending ladder. The drums appeal to Lenina, who notices they are like the ones for "Orgy-porgy." Men sing, then women. Suddenly monsters leap out dancing and whirling, people shriek, and a figure dispenses snakes from a wooden chest. Then there is a dance and a ritual with the snakes. A boy begins to walk in a circle around the snakes, and he is whipped by a man in a coyote mask. An eagle and a man on a cross watch the ceremony until the people, snakes, and beaten boy are gone. Then the square is empty. Lenina is sobbing uncontrollably.

Then a blond boy, dressed like an Indian, appears and speaks to them in English. He complains that he could have made a better sacrifice than the boy Palowhtiwa, whose blood lies now on the ground. Yet the people will not choose him because of his complexion. Lenina is surprised that he actually wants to be hit with the whip. The boy explains that he would like to do it for Pookong and Jesus. Then he is overcome by Lenina's appearance, and she notices that he is handsome.

The boy explains to Bernard that he and his mother, Linda, are strangers in the Reservation, that she came from the Other Place with a man named Tomakin who was the boy's father. The man went back without Linda and the boy was born there, in Malpais. Bernard is intensely interested in this story.

The boy takes Bernard and Lenina to his mother's hovel on the outskirts of the pueblo. Linda appears in the dress of a squaw, with teeth missing, fat, ragged, and filthy, and hugs the appalled Lenina vigorously. Linda is overcome with emotion. She is delighted to see what she never thought she would see again — signs of the civilization that she was forced to leave. In a rush of remembered images from the world outside and the world of the Reservation, Linda tells her story. She tells about having John in shame, about being without *soma* but assisted by the man Popé who brought *mescal*, about her inability to teach cleanliness or exercise it, about her inadequacy in a world lacking specialization, about being persecuted for having many men. Linda says that John is particularly sensitive about her having men and that John thinks like the Indians. Meanwhile John and Bernard go outside and talk.

Commentary

In literary tradition, going back to the most sacred literatures in the world, passages in which major illuminations or insights occur often involve a journey up a mountain, where a sacred moment is witnessed, sometimes by people who have no way of comprehending the significance of the moment at all. Chapter 7 contains a moment of power that makes the rituals of the Brave New World pale beside it. The snake ritual of the Indians with its human sacrifice may seem to resemble "Orgy-porgy" at first, but the resemblance only adds to the mighty differences. The sacred moment of the ritual is bracketed by revelations of filth to those who cannot belong. Before the ritual Lenina is confronted only by the alien picture of another people, with whom she had not the slightest thing in common. After the ritual she comes face to face with the mirror image of herself made a part of the landscape she hates, in the figure of Linda. The sacred ritual not only occurs on a mesa, or flat top of a mountain in the middle of a plain, but in the very centre of the pueblo planted there. Bernard and Lenina do not comprehend the ritual; they only react to its power. Lenina's tears are the first signs of her humanity. Her outburst is like her terror in the face of the storm while over the Channel earlier, only here there is no escape.

Huxley carefully constructed the chapter so that the distinction between the world outside the mesa and that on top of it is clear. Halfway up the side of the mesa an eagle swoops by them and they see a pile of bones. The full sunlight and the flat deck of stone are elements of sacred space. This is an area of old age, disease, filth, generation, and savagery. Yet here is also a theatre where an entire community joins in a rite that combines the Indian and Christian rituals to make the rain come and the corn grow.

Just what the ritual means, in detail, is not as important as feeling that here, human passion is possible in ways that are impossible in the Brave New World. Participation in the sacrifice, not only psychically but, in the case of John, physically, becomes one of the high points of life. Characteristically, Huxley contrasts the power of the ritual with the power of the ridiculous figure of Linda. Her likeness in attitudes to Lenina is intended to throw all the new-world values into high relief. Taken out of the comfortable whole of her world of shallowness and made to work her way into the old world, she has simply failed utterly. She has become a hopeless outcast — a whore, a drunkard, a slovenly and unclean beast, wrapped up in self-pity, with no way of dealing with a child of any kind, much less an intelligent boy like John.

Just as Linda and Lenina are meant to be compared and contrasted with each other, so are Bernard and John. Both are outcasts from their societies on physical as well as emotional grounds. Both have reservations about sexuality. Neither can participate as he wishes in the rituals of his culture. Both are victims of self-pity. Both are intelligent, but neither is capable of thinking himself out of his situation. Both are curiously attracted to Lenina.

John's desire to be the sacrificial centre of his culture will have unfortunate consequences later, when he is transplanted to the Brave New World. If he were only a product of Linda and her rugged, earthy friends, like Popé, he would simply not be what he is. John's substitute for sleep-teaching is his Shakespeare. Although this has not been made explicit yet, Huxley draws almost every moral statement by the boy and almost every allusion, from the works of William Shakespeare. "The multitudinous seas incarnadine," for example, is purposely overdone by Huxley, and in his time it would have been recognized immediately. It is great fun on one level to see the boy straining to use the world view of Shakespeare to explain his world. But Huxley is making a point about learning this way too. Shakespeare is just not enough.

CHAPTER 8

Summary
Bernard probes John's memory in an attempt to know what produced him, and he gains a series of sharp scenes from the boy's past. John begins with the earliest scene he can recall and works forward in time.

The first scene is John's memory of falling asleep to his mother's new-world songs, only to be rudely awakened by a hideous man with black ropes of hair, who was trying to make his mother do something. The man finally threw John out of the room and fastened the door. John could not get his mother to answer him through the door.

John remembers later going with his mother to a large room where the Indian women did their weaving. He was placed among the children to play. His mother joined in the work, but soon there was trouble because she broke something. She called the people savages, and she and John left. At their house the man named Popé was waiting with a gourd full of powerful liquid. When Popé left, John could not awaken his drunken mother.

Popé often brought the liquid *mescal*. John hated Popé and all the other men who came to visit his mother. One day in winter, John was horrified to find his mother being beaten with a whip by three Indian women. When he tried to help her, he was pushed down and beaten too. Later he tried to find out from his mother why the women had been cruel. She, not understanding it herself, tried to explain, but then struck out at the boy repeatedly. Finally she took him in her arms.

John recalls his mother sleeping, drunk, and sick.

The happiest times for John were those when his mother reminisced about the Other Place. She spoke of flying, of listening to music from a box, of everybody being happy, of everybody belonging to everyone else, and so on. John was also enthralled by stories told by one of the old men of the pueblo, of the great Transformer of the World, of Awonawilona, Jesus and Pookong, and of the other spirits of this world. John blended the two traditions while lying in bed, dreaming of both.

The men continued to come to Linda, and John was taunted by the other boys who called his mother dirty names. Once they threw a rock that cut his cheek, and the blood from the wound covered him.

Linda taught John how to read, first by drawing on the wall, and then by giving him her technical manual from the Embryo Store.

John was taunted for being dressed in rags, but he consoled himself in the knowledge that he could read. He turned to read more, the more the others taunted him. When he asked Linda about what words like "chemicals" meant, he did not receive satisfactory answers. More satisfactory than Linda's answers were those given by the old men of the pueblo, about the nature of the universe.

Soon after his twelfth birthday John discovered a book he had never seen before on the floor of his bedroom — *The Complete Works of William Shakespeare*. Linda told him that Popé found the book in a chest of the Antelope Kiva. John opened the book and found that the words there spoke more strongly to him than any in the pueblo culture.

John was particularly struck by passages that illuminated his hatred of Popé. One day he found Popé in bed with his mother. He remembered words from *Hamlet*, seized a knife, and stabbed Popé. But Popé, though cut, only held him until he began to cry.

Old Mitsima taught John how to work clay, and promised to teach him how to make a bow.

After witnessing a wedding for Kothlu and Kiakimé, John was moved by old Mitsima's words, "It is finished." When Linda denigrated the service John ran off, since he had loved Kiakimé himself.

When they met near the Antelope Kiva for the ceremony of manhood, John was ruthlessly excluded, even stoned. Alone outside, he was impressed with his loneliness even more than by his bruises and blood.

Bernard is especially moved by this admission of the boy's loneliness, and confesses to the boy that he, too, feels alone. The boy is surprised that anyone in the Other Place should be alone. He says that when the other boys were sent out to spend the night on the mountains, he too went separately and dreamed his own dream. He will not tell Bernard what he dreamed, but he does tell about another time when he stood against a rock in the middle of the day with his hands outstretched like Jesus, just to feel what he must have felt on the cross. After a time, he fainted, and now he shows Bernard the scar. Bernard is disgusted on account of his conditioning. He changes the subject to a plan he has been formulating. He suggests that John return with him to the Other Place. When John asks whether Linda can come too, Bernard realizes that the ugly woman may be an asset. To John's question whether he and Lenina are married, Bernard laughingly says no. John, alive with visions of the Other Place says, "O brave new world," but he is cautioned from a too-hasty conclusion by Bernard.

Commentary

The sequence of stories told by John to Bernard evokes a sense of what it must have been like to live as an outcast among the inhabitants of the pueblo. John's life has been one of estrangement and alienation. He has been on the outside of two worlds — the world of his parents, which he has never seen and knows only through Linda's incoherent memories, and the pueblo world, which he understands in the fragments he can gather from a foreign tongue and in those events from which he cannot be excluded. His refuge is his literacy. Yet he is self-taught, and much of what he learns from literature he misapplies.

The home Linda creates for John is sordid at best. She is a notorious whore and drunkard. She can do nothing except feel sorry for herself because her culture prepared her only for menial work at a limited job. She cannot sew or keep a decent house. She is disgusted by her son and ashamed to have borne him naturally. Her slovenliness is not excused by her surroundings, and Huxley gives little opportunity for pitying her. The focus is clearly on John's struggle for meaning in the world from which she has, by her nature, shut him out.

John's imaginative world is formed by the old mythologies — both the Indian folklore and Christian folklore, by Linda's tales of the Other Place, by Shakespeare's poetry, and by his own fertile imagination. Pain defines his memories. In most of his stories pain is the central memory — culminating in his attempt to feel what Jesus felt on the cross. By nature John experiments. By nature he rises above suffering to meaning.

Old Mitsima is an exception to a world that ignores him. Popé is a horrid father figure, laughing at John's pain. But where Popé violates his mother and makes home a bed of pain, Mitsima opens possibilities for John that would not otherwise materialize. But even Mitsima cannot stop the course of nature when John's beloved is married to an Indian rival.

John's experience is saturated by evil views on human sexuality. He is subject to every young man's desires, but Linda's performances make him disgusted with physical contact. John's attraction to Kiakimé and to Lenina, even his identification with the chaste Miranda, indicates the ideal he holds of perfect womanhood. The formative aversion to sex will haunt him to his end.

Huxley has clearly created Bernard and John as doubles. While Bernard listens to John, he sympathizes with the history of alienation. Bernard's ability to identify with the young man is not complete, since Bernard has been too thoroughly conditioned and since Bernard has other motives for listening than sympathy. In fact, Bernard's plan to use John for his own purposes distinguishes the two completely on the moral plane. Bernard does not think for a minute what the consequences of John's returning will be for John. He only thinks about his own predicament and the embarrassment of his boss, the Director.

Ironically, only after John tells Bernard the secret of his "crucifixion" does Bernard change the subject. Just as Bernard shied away from Helmholtz's confession of the emptiness of the new world earlier, here he shies away from an important revelation about the tragic character of John. The image of sacrifice will become a reality later, when John hangs himself in the new world he is so eager to see.

Bernard and John are different not only because they are misfits in different cultures. They are different in their inmost characters too. If Bernard has been conditioned by imperfect bottling techniques, John has been ennobled by natural birth in a natural setting. Huxley seems to imply a problem beyond the particular breeding program in the new world. He implies that natural childbirth makes stronger specimens than Alpha-Pluses. Compare John with Helmholtz or Bernard — though only a boy, he bests them.

John's attraction to Shakespeare is a tribute to the power of the Renaissance playwright's language. It is unsettling that Popé is to be thanked for providing the text for John. Also the ancient book comes from the Antelope Kiva, which is associated throughout the account of the pueblo with secret rites and mysteries. Although nobody can read it, the book is a treasure from the Kiva, transmitted to John not by a schoolmaster but by one of the darkest figures in the book. That John thinks that he must kill Popé on the basis of a passage from the book compounds the irony of its transmission. Popé brings *mescal* for Linda, and Shakespeare for John. Where Linda's escape from the pueblo has for years been *mescal*, John's has increasingly been the book and his imagination.

Bernard's friend, Helmholtz, and John have in common an interest in language. But Helmholtz lacks the passion and the context to make language live. John, on the other hand, has the passion and feels the piercing words, yet is so involved in living Shakespeare that he cannot use his knowledge to protect himself. Shakespeare, Huxley seems to say, is far more powerful than advertising lingo to probe the depths of the human condition.

Huxley does not idealize life on the Reservation. Society there has its rituals and taboos. John is who he is because he is an outcast, not because he is a perfect Indian boy. Alienation seems to be the origin of identity. Pain and self-analysis are, for Huxley, necessary evils.

CHAPTER 9

Summary

After their full day at the Reservation, Lenina collapses into a *soma* dream world and Bernard stays up late into the night perfecting a plan. Since Lenina will not awaken until five the next afternoon, Bernard has time to go to Santa Fé to do business. He flies to Santa Fé and, after getting through the many secretaries, speaks directly with Mustapha Mond to request that he be permitted to bring John and Linda back to London with him. The World Controller wires immediately to the Warden that Bernard's wishes in this matter are to be fulfilled. Then, satisfying himself that the Warden has received the orders, Bernard relaxes for a while.

John arrives at the rest-house to see Bernard but does not find him. He throws a stone through a window and goes through Lenina's green suitcase, delighting in the smell of her perfume. He discovers Lenina asleep and beautiful on a bed in the adjacent room. Enraptured, he kneels beside her bed and recites poetry in her praise. He overcomes the desire to touch her, and is repulsed by the impulse to pull down the zipper that holds her bedclothes around her. He sees her as a pure virgin. He hears a plane coming, vaults through the window and races to meet Bernard.

Commentary

This short chapter provides a strong contrast between Bernard and John. The link between them is Lenina, who has opted for a *soma* holiday as an antidote to the sights of the pueblo. Bernard, knowing the effects of the drug, immediately puts in motion his plan by calling the World Controller, Mustapha Mond. His plea to return with the two "specimens" is based on their being of "sufficient scientific interest." No mention is made of the effects such a transfer might have on the two individuals or anyone else. Bernard spends no time deliberating on this or speaking of it with Mond. Typically, Bernard spends his free time after setting the plan in motion enjoying the new world's luxuries.

While Bernard is enjoying himself, so is John. Like a savage, he has gained access to the rest-house by throwing a stone through a window. Again like a savage, he goes through Lenina's clothes, only dimly aware of the libidinous impulses behind his actions. Yet when he discovers his sleeping beauty he drops his savagery and becomes primly civilized. He treats Lenina as if she were enshrined. He is guilty not only about having the impulses natural to mankind, but about entering in the first place. Clearly John's ambivalence about sexuality is established. On the one hand, he is a natural savage. On the other hand, he has a romanticized ideal of womanhood that bears no critical examination. She had invited him to visit them, but then she had thoughtlessly gone to sleep.

Ironically, on the bed, she is like John's mother Linda, in that scene of his earliest recollection. Like Linda, Lenina reacted to strong aversion by seeking the oblivion of a tonic. Huxley set up the parallel between Linda and Lenina early in the visit. John does not realize the similarities, but he is attracted to Lenina much as to a replica of his early visions of his mother as of a lover. Yet John cannot see in Lenina the tendencies that made his mother what she is. And he firmly suppresses any impulses in himself that remind him of Popé.

Huxley has given John more than imaginative sensitivity. He has given him higher sense perceptions than the others, as well. John savours smells and listens deeply. He has a delight in touching, and he records every detail of the wonderful things he sees in Lenina's luggage. John thinks like a poet. Lenina's likeness to a dangerous and beautiful bird; and his own likeness to a wet dog shaking its ears — these are symbolic associations not made by inhabitants of the other world.

Playfully Huxley makes a fly buzz around the sleeping Lenina, perhaps as a symbol of lurking sexuality. Then, accentuating the image, the distant sound of Bernard's plane is that of a fly too — then a wasp. Huxley uses the heightened sensitivity of John to enliven his own use of language, moving in a progression of images — fly, bird, dog, fly, wasp, plane — to chart the imagination of the savage boy and to give in image form an impression of the dangers these people pose for him.

CHAPTER 10

Summary

At twenty-seven minutes past two in London at the Fertilizing Room of the Central London Hatchery a host of usual events are taking place in the massive building: fertilizing, bokanovskifying, decanting, feeding, sleep-teaching, playing, and so on. Yet the Director tells Henry Foster that at two-thirty in this room he will make a public example of Bernard Marx. To Henry Foster's hypocritical observation that Marx does his job well enough, the Director replies that any individual can be remade — but society must be protected from a man whose behaviour would destroy it.

Bernard arrives on time, and the Director calls everyone's attention to him in a loud voice. In what is probably a prepared speech he denounces Bernard Marx as an "enemy of Society," "a conspirator against Civilization itself." He announces his decision to send Bernard to Iceland as a punishment and, impressively, asks Bernard whether there is any reason that the punishment should not be carried out immediately. To everyone's surprise, Bernard says he has a reason and opens the door to admit it.

Linda enters in all her filth and disfigurement. When Bernard identifies the Director, Linda calls out endearments to "Tomakin," and, frustrated, she lunges forward to embrace him. Over the Director's embarrassment, and over the increasing laughter of the assembled workers, Linda tells him that he made her have a baby and that she was its mother. At this news, the crowd becomes silent, and Linda breaks away from her Tomakin to call forth John. John strides in on moccasined feet and kneels before the Director, saying, "My father!" This "obscenity" brings forth howls of laughter from everyone. The Director, totally humiliated, covers his face with his hands and rushes out of the room.

Commentary

This short but dramatic chapter has one overriding function: to bite the biter. The Director, expecting his moment of triumph over the recalcitrant Bernard Marx, is instead defeated by his would-be adversary. Where he had carefully orchestrated Marx's total humiliation before the best and brightest persons in Society, his own humiliation was engineered.

Huxley has heightened the irony of this unexpected reversal by setting it in the Fertilizing Room. The joke arises from the fact that the Director formerly violated society's taboo by fertilizing an egg inside Linda. And because of her hideous looks, even an affair with her, on ordinary new-world terms, seems grotesque. The reader has been prepared for the impact of the revelation of this obscenity. It was only a matter of how it would be done. Linda alone would have been uproarious, but incomplete. The proof of the Director's deed could not rest upon her word but required the fruit of the unnatural union. Of course, the feelings of Linda and John are not examined. Bernard has staged the event to save himself. And, in justice, the tactic is good retribution. But significant pathos is built up in Linda's pathetic attempt to communicate with the man who caused her fall into a nightmarish world, and in John's noble gesture before the father he has never seen.

Comedy arises not from Linda's and John's disappointment but from the use of society's laws against the supposed upholder of those laws. The Director, pretending to be the pious judge, is in fact a hypocrite. Because he is so much a part of his societal role — and so little else — he cannot recover from this indignity. He is, in effect, destroyed.

Huxley's ironies go deeper, as usual, since Bernard becomes the unmasker of the Director. The supposed rebel ends up using the societal norms against which he rebelled to defend himself. And the workers who laugh, laugh at a process they themselves labour at, as their life's work. They betray the values their society as a whole has forfeited.

CHAPTER 11

Summary

All upper-caste London now wants to see John, but Linda is merely an obscenity, with an appearance that would make a person sick. Linda now returns to her *soma*, taking increasingly larger doses to maintain a constant state of oblivion. Her doctor confides to Bernard that such doses will kill her in a month or two. When John objects that the *soma* will shorten his mother's life, the doctor explains that each *soma* experience is an eternity. So Linda spends her days on holiday surrounded by radio and television and perfumed scents. The doctor is gratified to have the opportunity of witnessing a specimen of senility.

Only through Bernard can John be seen. For a while he basks in the light of his new role — men and women alike think highly of him. Bernard boasts of his new fame and his female conquests to a gloomy Helmholtz. Success goes to Bernard's head. He becomes reconciled in every way to the world which formerly he detested. Yet he goes about unguardedly criticizing anything and anyone he wishes. People begin to talk about his unorthodoxy, saying that next time there will not be a Savage to save him.

Bernard escorts the Savage on a tour of civilized life in all its aspects. Assuming the air of a World Controller, Bernard tries to impress everyone. The Savage, however, is not easily impressed.

In his reports to Mustapha Mond, Bernard Marx oversteps his bounds, not only assuming airs but also attempting to lecture the powerful Controller about the social order. Mond is at first angry at his tone, then mirthful. He resolves to teach Bernard Marx a lesson — later.

Given a tour of a factory of lighting-sets for helicopters, the Savage is overcome with nausea at the sight of the orderly workers and the tone of the Human Element Manager as he discusses the efficiency of work. He retches.

Bernard writes in his report that the Savage will not take *soma* and that he objects to his mother's remaining permanently on *soma* holiday. He also remarks on the Savage's attachment to his mother — an attachment he finds abnormal.

At Upper School, Eton, the Provost and Head Mistress give a tour. The Provost tells John that students here are not twins, but that each comes from a separate egg. Bernard arranges a date with the Head Mistress. They visit a class on elementary relativity for Alpha-Double-Pluses, then one on geography for Beta-Minuses. In geography the students laugh at a film of *Penitentes* whipping each other. John is bewildered by their laughter. Meanwhile Bernard places his arm around the Head Mistress's waist. Later when they visit the rooms where hypnopaedic lessons are stored, John asks whether the students read Shakespeare. The Provost exclaims that "We don't encourage them to indulge in any solitary amusements." The Provost explains about a bus just back from Slough Crematorium, where death-conditioning takes place.

Bernard makes a telephone call at the Television Corporation's factory at Brentford, and the Savage watches the Main Day-Shift line up to get their *soma* rations.

Lenina tells Fanny that she is to take the Savage to the feelies tonight. Lenina has shared in the celebrity surrounding the Savage. Many times she has been asked what it is like to go to bed with a savage, but she has replied that she does not know. And to her regret, she does not. She likes the Savage and senses that he likes her, and she is bewildered that he has been reticent.

At the feelies there is a delight for each sense. First, smell is given a thorough workout in the dark. Then hearing is treated to machine music. For the eye and sense of touch, Lenina tells the Savage to grasp the metal knobs on his chair. They and the rest of the audience experience, as if at first-hand, a romance between a gigantic negro male and a blonde female. The negro, on account of a helicopter accident, goes antisocial and abducts the blonde. She is saved after three weeks by three heroic Alphas, who become her lovers. Lenina is deeply moved by the experience. The Savage ruthlessly represses his desire and ignores her need. He says, to her shock, that the film is base and ignoble. When the taxicopter reaches her apartment house, he surprises her again by departing suddenly instead of going inside. Back in his own room he takes down *Othello*, which is about a black man like the one in the feelie, and reads it. Meanwhile Lenina has dried her eyes and decided to take three tablets of *soma*.

Commentary

The overriding reason that no one wishes to see Linda is,

symbolically, her appearance. For in the Fordian scheme of things, there is no age or grotesque deformity. Bernard himself had been shunned because of his differences from other members of his class. But Linda's obesity, bad teeth, and complexion are another matter. Just as no one wants to see her (except her son), she does not care to see anyone else. She embraces the drug that was unavailable to her during her stay at the Reservation, even though the size of her doses means that she will die soon.

Dr. Shaw, as the representative of the medical profession in the novel, defends her *soma*-suicide on the grounds that she has no useful purpose in society anyway. After all, she cannot work, and she makes a fuss when she is not given her *soma*. He is thankful to have a chance to observe senility because up until the moment of death, people in the Brave New World remain young. One failure of the medical technology available is that it cannot reverse the process of ageing.

The chapter is focussed on two main figures — Bernard Marx and the Savage. In the chapter Bernard becomes a boastful, swell-headed man, eager to embrace a society that no longer seems to exclude him. The Savage, in contrast, remains detached and critical of everything he sees. In effect the Savage becomes the hero of the novel at this point. Bernard falls to the lowest forms of delights and even treats the World Controller badly. Bernard establishes the grounds for his later expulsion by forgetting wholly who he is and what his limits are. The Savage asserts rather than relinquishes his morality.

The Savage's reaction to his tour of the Electrical Equipment Corporation is a summary of his view of the new technology. He recites once again the words, "O brave new world," and retches violently. This retching to purify himself is repeated later. Bernard has no sympathy whatever for the boy. He finds it curious that the Savage should wish to see his disfigured mother.

At Eton the film showing the *Penitentes* at Acoma foreshadows the final chapter of the book, when those who observe the Savage imitate the flagellants of the film. The Savage is bewildered that the students should laugh at the penitents, and the Provost shows his own lack of humanity by stating that the scene is funny. This film, like the feely later in this chapter, relates directly to the plot. How people react to it defines their tastes and sensibilities. That this is the school which produces the training for the best minds of this society suggests a degeneracy of education that is irredeemable.

The Savage's perspective throughout the chapter is that of the overview. He sees not one but multitudes standing in line for *soma*. The *soma* pills are distributed in containers he calls "caskets," and earlier he had observed the bus-load of students back from a lesson in death-conditioning. Through the Savage's eyes the Brave New World becomes increasingly menacing. The mechanical nature of the work, the mindless nature of work and play, the death-like sterility of the culture are in the foreground, while John's mother slowly kills herself with society's answer to its own emptiness — *soma*. In the song Lenina sings to Fanny, the words *soma* and *coma* rhyme. This is not idle comedy. It is as if all experiences — in this case love — reduce to *soma*, which produces a coma-like state.

The date of John and Lenina is, for Lenina, an opportunity of having the Savage sexually for the first time. Her disappointment signals the Savage's firm adherence to his values, even though he suspects that his view of Lenina as chaste may be wrong. The feelies give all the participants the occasion to think that they have gone to the limits of sensual experience. The central extravaganza is *Three Weeks in a Helicopter*, a grotesque parody of Shakespeare's play, *Othello*, as John suspects. Huxley has a lot of fun making a plot that in a few rude details resembles the play. But more than the travesty on the screen, the reactions of the participants, particularly Lenina, and the content of the work leave no doubt about the society's banality and thirst for exotic sexuality through artificial means. Lenina is aroused by the experience, ready for John's embraces. He, on the other hand, is repulsed by the film and by her emerging lust. John's behaviour, by this society's standards, is criminally deviant. Earlier Huxley established the equivalency of new-world *soma* with John's Shakespeare. In keeping with that suggestion, Lenina seeks refuge in *soma* while John pulls out his Shakespeare after their date.

John cannot accept the Brave New World's patterns of work or play. He retreats here, just as he used to at the Reservation, to his book. Here, as, there his imaginative interaction with reading defines his separateness and even his alienation from society. The values he represents are wholly unintelligible to members of the Brave New World, and increasingly he becomes more than just an island of morality. John becomes a necessarily tragic hero in a world even more fallen than the one he left behind.

CHAPTER 12

Summary
Bernard begs John to emerge to meet the distinguished guests he has invited to a party, but the Savage refuses indignantly, cursing in Zuñi. Finally Bernard has to tell the assemblage that the Savage will not appear. The guests are outraged, and they vent their spleen by lashing out at Bernard. The Arch-Community-Songster speaks for everyone when he solemnly makes the sign of the sacred T over Bernard and says he should mend his ways. Afterwards he departs with Lenina in tow. When his guests have left, Bernard drowns his sorrows in *soma*. Meanwhile in his room the Savage reads *Romeo and Juliet*.

Mustapha Mond censors a brilliant paper with the title "A New Theory of Biology," and considers the damage that might be done to society if people were to think that life has a higher purpose than the maintenance of well-being. His hypocrisy is revealed in his knowledge that things could be different from what they are.

While John reverently mouths Shakespearean lines and thinks of Lenina, the Arch-Community-Songster dallies with her himself.

After the shock of the party, which reversed all of his expectations, Bernard is back to his old embittered self. The Savage notices his change of mood and says he prefers the honesty of his present attitude. Bernard, even though he senses the truth of the Savage's insight, plots little revenges against him. Unable to strike at powerful figures like the Arch-Community-Songster, Bernard turns against his friends, the Savage and Helmholtz. Helmholtz forgives him and listens sympathetically to his problems.

Later Bernard learns that Helmholtz is in trouble with the authorities: he recites as an example of propaganda a poem he wrote about being alone and was reported by his students to the Principal. Bernard sees why — the students were confronted with a direct contradiction to their lessons about the evil of solitude.

Helmholtz and the Savage like one another instantly. They enjoy sharing Shakespeare, much to Bernard's jealousy. Bernard enjoys interrupting their readings with rude allusions to society. Yet Helmholtz himself is overcome with laughter over a perfectly serious passage from *Romeo and Juliet* because he knows nothing about mothers, fathers, and daughters. Helmholtz proves that he is inescapably bound up in his own world. The Savage, indignant, puts the book away.

Helmholtz tells the Savage that the reason that Shakespeare could write powerfully is the "many insane, excruciating things" he had to write about. Now it would be ridiculous to write about fathers and mothers and getting excited about whether to have a girl or boy or not. Helmholtz says he does not know what the Brave New World can hold as a substitute.

Commentary

The Savage has turned from *Othello* to *Romeo and Juliet*. His refusal to be exhibited by Bernard marks a turning point for both of them. And because Bernard is again his old disgruntled self, he can turn again to his friend Helmholtz. By this means the three — Bernard, Helmholtz, and the Savage — form a curious triangular friendship. And Huxley has the opportunity to contrast Helmholtz's propaganda techniques with Shakespeare's poetry.

Characteristically, Bernard exhibits jealousy at the new friendship of Helmholtz and the Savage. But although Helmholtz is considered a rebel for his poetry of solitude, he is so much a product of his society that he cannot take the old customs that underpin the action of the old plays seriously. Shakespeare could write because he lived in a world quite different from the Brave New World. The failure of literature in the new world is the failure of life too. Helmholtz vaguely senses this deeper failure in his admission that he knows of no substitute for the material of *Romeo and Juliet*.

The pathetic form of the Savage's rhapsodic reading of "she doth teach the torches to burn bright" is immediately followed by the image of the golden T on Lenina's bosom shining while it is fondled by the Arch-Community-Songster. Lenina is far from the ideal figure worshipped by the Savage. While the Savage sings her praises, she is about to take *soma* and have the Songster.

Hardship and conflict produce the friendship that lasts to the end of the book. Each of the three men has experienced rejection and feels alienated from society. Bernard and Helmholtz have had recent failures. The Savage has recently decided not to be seen at the whim of others. In spite of the pain the men cause each other — or perhaps because of it — they become fast friends. There are limits to friendship. The limits are defined by the cultures from which the men come. Bernard and Helmholtz are post-Fordians; the Savage is a throwback to earlier ages.

Bernard's fall from his own pride is similar to the Director's. Both are suffering from exalted views of their positions in society. Both are brought low by the Savage. In the case of the Director, the Savage makes an expected appearance. In the case of Bernard, he does not make an expected appearance. For both the Director and Bernard, disgrace means exclusion from society. Fortunately for Bernard, he is not a Director. He is also fortunate that he has two friends. In literary tradition, *hubris*, or blinding pride about one's place in the world, causes tragedy. So far *hubris* is comic, but from the point at which the Savage excludes society, a tragic *hubris* develops. It becomes terrifying because the Savage's isolation is very complete and very serious. There are no hooks of affection for him in the Brave New World except for what Lenina represents. The theme of exile, hinted at in the *soma* experience of Linda and in the flight of Tomakin, intersects the theme of alienation.

CHAPTER 13

Summary

Henry Foster asks Lenina for a date and notices that she is sad. He suggests that she see a doctor, but she has her mind on John. In her disorientation Lenina forgets to give one embryo a sleeping sickness injection. Later this omission will cause the death of the person formed by it. In the Changing Room Lenina confesses to Fanny that she wants one man — John. She says she has tried *soma* and other men but she still wants him. Fanny advises her to take John by force at once.

Hoping that Helmholtz will arrive, John is surprised to find Lenina at his door, dressed marvelously. They sit down, and while John speaks admiringly Lenina draws closer to him until he is forced to scramble to his feet to escape. The Savage explains that at Malpais, one had to bring the beloved the skin of a mountain lion or a wolf when marriage was intended. He asks what he should do for her. To his suggestion that he sweep the floor, Lenina launches into an explanation that there are others to do that sort of work. In desperation John blurts out that he loves her, but he then tells her that at home the custom is to promise to live together always. Lenina thinks that a horrible idea. She knows nothing about virginity or the rest of his ideas.

Understanding only that he says he loves her, Lenina throws her arms around him and kisses him. Recalling the feely they saw together, John tries to escape. He thinks she has gotten the hint when she removes her belt and unzips her clothes. Finally clad only in shoes, socks and hat, she advances to take him, backs him against a wall, and entreats him to take her. Instead he turns ferocious and brutally thrusts her away, threatening to kill her. He slaps her naked flesh as she bounds for the safety of the bathroom. Raving mad and spouting quotations from his beloved Shakespeare, John storms about outside. He passes her clothes through the ventilator above the door. Only when the telephone rings and John departs to find his mother does Lenina escape.

Commentary

The thirteenth chapter is unlucky from two standpoints. First, Lenina and the Savage reveal their inmost thoughts about their love and clash violently because of their different attitudes. Second, John is only distracted from his ravings about Lenina's being a whore by news that his mother is badly off and has been moved.

Lenina's love sickness is abnormal in her culture. The cure prescribed by Fanny is simple: take the boy any way you can. This advice is unfortunate since neither woman realizes what is going through John's mind. Lenina narrowly escapes being murdered on account of her bad judgement. The Savage reveals his violent feelings and the blindness and destructiveness possible when his morality has been outraged. Love's sacrifice holds no meaning for Lenina — she cannot understand the lover's need to be heroic or to be degraded or to have a virginal companion. The conversation between the two is anything but communication because they will not attempt to understand each other.

Both Lenina and John are in a situation for which their backgrounds have not prepared them. Lenina resorts to a direct approach only when she has become ill by thinking solely of John. Yet she laughs when John tells her that it is customary in Malpais to promise to be faithful to one person. Lenina may feel the need to possess John, but not beyond a single experience. On the other hand John can spout poetry about his beloved, but for him she is only an abstraction, like the words on a page. She is not flesh and blood but an ideal. Raised in a context where raw physicality was part of daily life, John is unable to accept the fact of sexuality at all. His madness indicates how radically estranged from reality he is. Ironically the naked advances of Lenina throw him into his frenzy, while word of his mother's impending death brings him out of his insanity. Lenina and Linda are again related in John's experience of women.

Shakespeare is used with bitter irony in this chapter to highlight John's madness. What John seems to have learned from Shakespeare is the tragedy of love and the romantic idealization of the beloved, but not the reality of love. John says he "loves" Lenina, but he does not know what the term means and he certainly does not know how she is likely to interpret his confession. Further, the only sensation like Lenina's kiss he has ever known is from the disgusting feely *Three Weeks in a Helicopter*, the memory of which strains him to the breaking point.

CHAPTER 14

Summary

The Savage arrives at the Park Lane Hospital for the Dying and visits his mother on Ward 81. There every effort is made to keep the atmosphere pleasant, complete with television and perfumes. The nurse who escorts him is embarrassed to discover that he is to visit his mother.

Linda is watching a tennis match on television. Other patients on the ward look young but are dying. The nurse leaves John with Linda. Linda seems to recognize John but immediately falls asleep. John remembers his mother and weeps at the memories, even the ones of the Other Place, which he has carefully separated from the realities he has witnessed. He is interrupted in his thoughts by streams of khaki-clad children who are quick to see that Linda is different from the other dying folk. They remark on her obesity and clamour around her until John boxes one of them on the ear.

The Head Nurse rebukes John, and he silently threatens her but returns to his mother. Now, however, he cannot recapture the train of memories of the good times. Now he remembers the ugliness. And Linda in her stupor mentions Popé. Frustrated, John tries to force his mother's recognition of him, but she only says Popé. Only when he shakes her does he interrupt her fantasy and cause her to name him. As if in response to the encroachment of reality, Linda seems not to be able to breathe. The Savage runs to tell that he has killed Linda, and indeed she has died. He sobs uncontrollably while the Head Nurse wonders what his display will do for the death-conditioning of the children around her. To obliterate the image the children are seeing, the Head Nurse offers chocolate éclairs. Five of the twins eat the pastries around the bed where Linda's body lies. John, angered by their asking whether she is dead, pushes one of them down so that he cries.

Commentary
Earlier in the book, mention of death-conditioning has prepared us for this scene. This chapter rounds out the picture of life in the Brave New World. Alongside the images of life being created at the Hatchery is this image of death. The Crematorium, the lessons, the tours, and the rest are part of the landscape. John is the only person who has the emotion called grief. Formerly even the sensitive Helmholtz considered it a waste to leave a corpse uncremated. Not only does John grieve, he grieves for his mother. In the new world the term "mother" is an obscenity. Further, the creature for whom he mourns is grotesque.

The most significant fact about Linda's death is its immediate cause. John, in forcing her identification of him, seems to have induced her death. In the dream world of *soma* she was safe. Only when awakened to the reality her son represents does she find it impossible to breathe. John and what he represents is a horror. He was the great interruption in her life. She was never able to accept him for what he was. Instead she neglected him while she indulged herself with Popé and *mescal*. Her identification of John with Popé is painful to John, and this triggers his need to be known for himself. In a way John takes revenge on Linda for having Popé, by killing her. In another way John shakes off once and for all a deep identification he had felt between himself and Popé.

The Head Nurse, like many other officials in the Brave New World, wishes only to preserve the decorum of her society. For her, grief is antisocial. For her, privacy is not to be tolerated even at the moment of death. For her, pastries used as bribes will obliterate bad memories. She is very like the Director and a host of other members of this society who seem to know better than they do. Her response to the genuine grief of John is the curt, "Can't you behave?"

Absorbed in his grief and in a host of other emotions aroused by witnessing his mother's death, John has no sympathy for the children who are being indoctrinated. Already he has signalled his disgust for the New World, and now his estrangement from it becomes even more complete than it was. With his disillusionment with Lenina and his final agony with his mother, John has no reason left for sympathy.

CHAPTER 15

Summary
The Savage shoulders his way through the staff of the Park Lane Hospital for the Dying. They are lined up waiting for their *soma* ration, and they object to his jostling them. John emerges from his grief to the realization of the employees' "swarming indistinguishable sameness." The Savage revolves in his mind with increasing venom, "O brave new world," as the ritual of *soma* distribution begins. At a pitch of emotion, John bellows for the crowd to stop and then begins to plead that they not take the "poison" that is *soma*. The Deputy Sub-Bursar needs to hear no more and picks up the telephone.

Bernard, meanwhile, cannot find the Savage anywhere, and while he and Helmholtz are considering alternatives, he receives a phone call that the Savage has gone mad at the hospital.

The Savage hurls abuse at the assembled crowd. He calls them slaves and babies. Then, seeing that they cannot comprehend him, he begins to hurl the *soma* boxes through a window opening onto the inner court of the Hospital. The crowd becomes furious and presses towards the Savage just as Bernard and Helmholtz arrive. Helmholtz struggles to be by the side of the Savage, where he tries to ward off the crowd. The Savage, having emptied the *soma* box, lifts it to the crowd while proclaiming their freedom from the drug.

At this critical moment the police arrive. Bernard fatuously yells for help as the police subdue the crowd with *soma* vapour, a Synthetic Music Box and anesthetic. Bernard is subdued with the anesthetic. Soon the entire crowd is reduced to kissing and embracing. New pills are brought out and the distribution is accomplished. Afterward the Sergeant takes the three "troublemakers" away.

Commentary

Bernard, Helmholtz, and the Savage have already been identified as rebels. This chapter makes them accomplices in one of the greatest crimes that can be committed in this new world — a major public disturbance. The Savage has demonstrated his violent nature in his treatment of Lenina and of the children, in the previous two chapters. Up to this point, however, he has not done anything to reform the citizens of this society. He strikes out at the lifeblood of the world — *soma*. By denying the people their drug of release and pleasure, the Savage also unleashes the savage fury in their souls — a fury that has been contained only by years of conditioning. Only now when social peace is jeopardized do the police appear, implying that just such eventualities as this riot are part of the new world. The police are so effective that their methods seem to have had more than rehearsals as their preparation.

The Savage, as always, thinks in terms of Shakespeare when he tries to make a speech, but he has never faced a crowd of Deltas before this. Instinctively action takes the place of words. And the motive for action is not really humanitarianism but "an intense overpowering hatred of these less than human monsters." He wants to make the creatures be free, whether they like it or not. But the Savage is right about the poisoning power of *soma*. Only *soma* makes life bearable. Without it there is misery beyond imagining.

The characters of the three friends — Bernard, Helmholtz, and the Savage, are once again distinguished by their acts before the crowd. The Savage is most demonstrative. He acts on impulse, with a courage that is greater than any other in the book. Helmholtz, like one of the Alphas in the feely, springs to the Savage's defense, though he never would have been able to do what the Savage did. Bernard only pretends to be helpful, by yelling while the police subdue the crowd. The power of the medicine is so great that Helmholtz and the Savage are on the point of tears from its use. To Bernard's credit, after being anesthetized and after being interrupted when trying to edge away afterwards, he acknowledges that Helmholtz and the Savage are his friends. The three are bound by this admission to share the punishment for their crimes.

CHAPTER 16

Summary

Bernard, Helmholtz, and the Savage are ushered into the World Controller's study. While Bernard and Helmholtz sit down, the Savage surveys the books and tapes in the room and is particularly interested in a massive book entitled *My Life and Work, by Our Ford.* When Mustapha Mond enters, he addresses only the Savage, stating that the Savage must not like civilization much. The Savage confesses that he does not, to Bernard's horror.

When the Savage discovers that the World Controller knows Shakespeare, he is very impressed. The works of Shake-speare are banned but the Controller is above the law. The Savage wants to know why the works are banned. The Controller says that they are old and that old things, particularly beautiful old things, are put aside so that the people will like new ones. Plays like *Othello* would not be understood, and besides writers like Helmholtz will never write anything like *Othello* because the new culture has no social instability, no families, and no frustrations now that *soma* is universal. The Controller chides the Savage for expecting Deltas to know about freedom or to understand *Othello*.

When Helmholtz admits that it is difficult to achieve great-ness in writing when there is nothing to say, the Controller equivocates by stating that now writers must use "the most enormous ingenuity." Then he launches into an apology for a world of superficial happiness, which is never as exciting or heroic as a world of pain and suffering. He then defends the

Bokanovsky groups, the foundation of society. To this the Savage poses a question: why not a society of Alpha-Double-Pluses? But the World Controller explains that such a society would be nothing but trouble. And the proof of this was the experiment on Cyprus where, in A.F. 473, twenty-two thousand Alphas were deposited. There strife followed and finally the survivors petitioned the World Controllers to resume government. Mustapha Mond states flatly that the model society is like an iceberg, with one-ninth above the water line, the rest below.

Mond explains that the new world society is designed for maximum happiness, with just the right balance of work and *soma*-induced relaxation. He defends the static society where nothing changes, and states that science is a possible enemy to stability. Both art and science lead to danger. Mond explains that he was formerly a physicist whose work became dangerous. He was given a choice — to be exiled to do his science or to become Controller. Clearly he chose the latter course. He tells the three men that they will be sent to an island just like the one he might have experienced.

At the thought of banishment to an island, Bernard breaks down and begs not to be sent. He blames the others for all the trouble and finally kneels down before the Controller, sobbing. The Controller orders that Marx be removed and given a *soma* vaporization. When he has been taken away, the Controller muses that Bernard should be happy to be sent to a place where the most interesting men and women in the world are.

Helmholtz asks why the Controller chose his position over going to the island, but he does not get a full answer. The Controller explains that Mass Production edged out truth (science) and beauty (art) and replaced them with universal happiness. The Nine Years' War marked the turning point in world history — and afterwards anything seemed preferable to the troubles that were caused by the old patterns of thought. The price for happiness is the loss of beauty and truth.

The Savage now confronts the Controller with the fact that he did not go to an island. The Controller answers that he chose to serve happiness and says that if the islands were not available, troublemakers would have to be exterminated.

The Controller gives Helmholtz a choice of islands. Helmholtz wants to go to an island with a bad climate to sharpen his sensibilities for writing. The Controller suggests the Falkland

Islands. Agreeing with this choice, Helmholtz departs to see how Marx is doing.

Commentary

The World Controller's power of persuasion was first demonstrated when he appeared before the Director of the London Hatchery's students, in Chapter 3, to explain a few details of history. He is a master of language and deceit. None of the three men brought before him are able to see through his smooth presentation. Clearly he sees the Savage as an interesting case — one he has studied through Marx's reports. The Savage lies outside the masterful controls of his all-embracing society. His title of World Controller seems deserved. He does control every situation. He has an answer for everything.

The Controller is almost a god within his society. Earlier he censored a brilliant scientist's report and consigned the writer to island isolation. Now he claims that he once was on the brink of being banished too. He delights in tasting forbidden knowledge — but also in exercising control. What he gave over was science and truth. What he gained in return was raw power. Now he lords over his world with impunity.

Among the forbidden things known to the Controller are Shakespeare and, probably, a host of other forbidden authors, the latest thought of every description, and the knowledge of history. He says he can accept a world where technology has been frozen and science has become a sterile discipline, a world which reduces all experience to a *soma* dream. Yet he does not use *soma*, and he actually enjoys the power that his knowledge of history gives him. If Ford claimed that history is bunk, Mond certainly knows and uses a lot of bunk to establish his sovereignty.

The Controller is the most dangerous man in the landscape because he has the intellect to know what is better, while holding the power to squelch what is better as a matter of "duty" in his service to happiness. Notice that when the Savage tries to pin him down about his choice to stay in society, the Controller changes his stance and asserts his power. The island is better than the death chamber, he says.

One further aspect of the Controller that bears scrutiny is his ability to vary his viewpoint depending on the people he addresses. He is one person in front of the Alpha students, another when alone considering Marx's correspondence, another with the three men, another when Marx has been carried away, and another with the Savage alone. He has identity only in terms of power. He does not take *soma*, does not associate with women, and seems to be as much on an island, in his isolation, as if he had been exiled to a real island.

Huxley, through the Controller, seems to give the new world a philosophical and even a scientific basis, and his power may for some even make him enviable. Yet at a few points Huxley lets his readers see through his mask: as when Mond mutters about the "tame animals" or when his oratory seems to be "almost up to synthetic standards." In short, Mond is a consummate hypocrite, a liar, and a fraud. He represents his society well — for he is as shallow as it is. In fact, he is the worst in his society since he has the tools to make other choices — any choices, and he cuts off the freedom to choose for a whole society.

The existence of islands which are communities for the misfits of the intelligentsia answers another question that the novel had left unanswered to this point. In order to keep society stable, not only police but prison-islands are necessary. The social fabric on every level must be artificially maintained. What seemed like an isolated problem in Marx's and Watson's alienation is so widespread that the world's islands have become havens, like the Savage Reservation, for malcontents. However, on the islands there are no traditions to fall back on, and the unrest during the experiment on Cyprus looms as a possibility on every one of them.

CHAPTER 17

Summary

When he is alone with the Controller, the Savage asks whether anything else besides beauty and truth (or art and science) had to be sacrificed for "happiness." Religion also was abandoned. The Controller takes from his safe the Bible and other religious works, and he says he does not give the people word about God because, as with *Othello*, they would not understand.

Mond reads a passage from Cardinal Newman about everyone being "God's property," then one from Maine de Biran about the sickness of old age. He concludes that in the modern world, religion is superfluous. God, he maintains, manifests himself in different ways for different times. At present, he manifests himself as an absence. When Mond says that people are conditioned to think of God, the Savage says that God is felt when people are alone. But, Mond replies, people are never alone now. Besides, man cannot be viewed as degraded unless you take a view from outside society. Within it, the new-world pleasures are wholly innocent. The Savage will not agree that values are relative but sees values as eternal and unchanging.

God becomes the centre of the Savage's argument. With God self-denial would be justified. But Mond sees belief in God as the beginning of instability and chaos. When the Savage argues that God is the basis of nobility and heroism, Mond counters that such values are no longer necessary in the new world order. Heroism, in fact, is a symptom of the failure of the social order. Christianity, for Mond, is revolution; *soma* is "Christianity without tears." But the Savage sees tears as necessary for value to exist. He is troubled that in the new world it is easy to do away with everything unpleasant.

Now the Savage thinks about his mother in her *soma* state and his father Tomakin in his *soma* state, and he states that civilization needs tears, that nothing costs enough here. When he asks Mond whether men don't need to live dangerously occasionally, Mond replies that the V.P.S. (Violent Passion Surrogate) treatments give the equivalent of fear and rage. Everything has been considered, and all passions can be gratified artificially.

The Savage now asserts his values: "I don't want comfort. I want God, I want poetry, I want real danger, I want freedom, I want goodness, I want sin." Mond says that the Savage is welcome to the agonies of life as the old way dictates.

Commentary

Now that the Controller and the Savage are alone together, they speak about the really essential lack in the new world order — God. For Mond, God is expressed by his absence. For the Savage, God is the basis for everything of value. For Mond, the old books spoke of truths that no longer apply because society is totally different from the one from which they evolved. For the Savage, verities do not change with every human age but persist until the end, always ennobling and always the same. The Controller withholds the word of God from the people because religion would destroy society. The Savage indignantly defends God as the source of all societal value. The contrast between these two is the contrast between the worlds, old and new, that have been presented in the novel. Notice that the argument is not God versus Ford, but God versus no God, or at least versus the absence of God. Throughout the novel, Christianity has been seen only in some rituals that have been carried over into a new mythological framework. In Fordian terms the cross has become the sacred T. In the Indian Reservation, Jesus joins Pookong. Where Shakespeare is found in a chest in the Kiva, the Bible is found in a safe in the Controller's office. Knowledge is everywhere in chains, under the pretext that it is dangerous to let it out among the people.

The arguments of the Controller become sharper in this chapter than the last. He seems very familiar with the heretical texts he opens and uses to show the useless ways of the past. But instead of allowing the Savage to savour the Bible itself, the Controller carefully brings the frame of reference back to Shakespeare. In Shakespeare there is no coherent theology, and the Savage must somehow deal with the ambivalences that his limited knowledge forces upon him. The Controller might at this time have given the Savage a way out of his plight. Instead he harbours his secret knowledge of the contents of the Bible, and the Savage remains ignorant. This chapter points out the limits of Shakespeare while it highlights the virtue of the Savage. The Savage endures the solecisms of the Controller and even articulates his beliefs better than ever before, because of the challenges presented to him.

The rights listed by the Controller as following from the Savage's ideas are the rights to a life as sordid as any in the Reservation. Indeed they catalogue the worst aspects of the life John knew before his transportation to the civilization he abhors. In a way John cannot escape his conditioning any more than Bernard can his. Yet John was a product not of Indian culture as much as his own imagination, shaped somewhat by Shakespeare and his broken home. Defined by pain instead of pleasure, John's world is in stark contrast to everything that Mond says he stands for.

CHAPTER 18

Summary

Helmholtz and Bernard come upon the Savage purging himself from the uncleanness of civilization with mustard and warm water. Helmholtz says they are leaving tomorrow morning. Bernard apologizes for the events of yesterday. The Savage says he went to see the Controller this morning to get permission to go to the islands with his friends, but the Controller denied the request because he wants the experiment to continue. The Savage says he, too, will go away tomorrow to a place where he can be alone.

The Savage chooses as his "hermitage" an old lighthouse on the crest of the hill between Puttenham and Elstead. He seeks a life of strict self-discipline, and he begins with a night of sleepless prayer. He regrets that the place he has chosen is beautiful, for he wishes to mortify himself. From his lighthouse he can see the skyscrapers of Guildford and the tower of Elstead, but his days are spent in glorious solitude — at first.

The expense money he received at his first arrival has gone for some basic supplies for survival outside the realm of humanity. The woods are full of game, and vegetables will grow in the place. Materials for making a bow and arrows are nearby, and when John begins to work, he sings.

Three Delta-Minus landworkers witness the Savage purging himself one day — whipping himself and retching. Then three days later the reporters come. While John is busy feathering his arrows, the fatuous reporter from *The Hourly Radio* tries to conduct an interview by turning himself into a walking transceiver. The unfortunate man, Primo Mellon, receives a tremendous kick from the Savage, but even this becomes instant news. Other reporters meet with increasingly violent receptions, and the Savage puts an arrow through the bottom of one helicopter, thus putting a damper on the reporters for a time.

Lenina's memory rises within him while he rests after working his garden plot. Her sensuality is repugnant to him, and he hurls himself into some spiky juniper bushes, then whips himself frenziedly. Unseen by the Savage, all this time Darwin Bonaparte, the Feely Corporation's expert big-game photographer, is making a film of his self-mortification. Twelve days later *The Savage of Surrey* bursts all over Western Europe. The afternoon following the evening of its release, John's solitude is invaded by scores of helicopters full of curious people. As they surround him, he threatens with his whip. The people chant that they want him to whip himself. Then another helicopter arrives, and Lenina steps out, with tears on her cheeks and her arms outstretched. The Savage races towards her and lashes her. Then he turns the whip on himself. When he does so, the assembled crowd, accustomed as they are to mindless imitation, begin to strike at each other. Then someone begins "Orgy-porgy," and they begin to dance. Only after midnight does the last of the helicopters leave. The next morning the Savage awakens and remembers — everything.

That evening another swarm of helicopters arrives with a new group of curious people. They find the Savage hanging just under the crown of the arch in the lighthouse.

Commentary

The tragic ending of the novel might have been prevented if Mustapha Mond, World Controller, had honoured the Savage's request to go with his friends to the islands. The Savage will not allow the "experiment" to continue but strikes out to find a space for solitude. Clearly this decision may have been foreseen by Mond, compounding his evil. What else was the Savage to do if he were to maintain his ideals?

The Savage's retreat is in part based on Henry Thoreau's experience at Walden Pond, but instead of making nature his study, the Savage mortifies himself. The Savage sings happily at work in his solitude, and he would blend into the natural surroundings well if he were not interrupted. But Thoreau and the Savage have no place in the modern order. The Savage is hunted down and made a celebrity because of his fierce desire for independence. His penitence, like that of the *Penitentes* in the film at Eton, is comic for the filmmaker Bonaparte and a font of ritual for the masses. One horror in the final scene with the dance is that the Savage has become the priest, the centre of the ritual turned inside out.

The likeness of the *Penitentes* film to *The Savage of Surrey* is not accidental. The Savage returns to his roots by engaging in the age-old ritual of his tribe. Disgusted by the Etonian students' laughter in the face of what was to him a most serious communal event, the Savage would be even more disgusted by the transformation of the religious purgation into the banal dance to "Orgy-porgy."

The last link to humanity for the Savage is his friendship for Bernard and Helmholtz. When they depart, he is essentially alone for the first time in his life. It is clear that he cannot ever have a friendship with Mustapha Mond, and his venomous attack on Lenina when she visits his refuge indicates that he wishes ruthlessly to expunge her memory.

The mass hysteria at the refuge is meant to be a mirror reflection of the mass hysteria at the Hospital for the Dying. There the Savage threw away *soma* and was attacked by the assembled Deltas. Here the mob takes away the Savage's solitude and is attacked by him. Both the Hospital and the lighthouse are scenes of death. Linda dies when her son awakens her to the reality of himself. John dies when he finds himself unable to deal with reality. For John, solitude is like *soma*, and nature is a benign companion. The fact that John's self-flagellation triggers an attempt by the masses to imitate his action indicates a deep and yet inarticulate need in the masses. Ironically John finally has the communal role he never had on the Reservation, but he cannot accept it. He does not sacrifice himself for an unworthy humanity as Jesus did. His death is sordid and prosaic. Where he dreamed of being Jesus on the cross and where he bitterly resented not being chosen to take the whip in the Indian ritual, he is unable to see a relation between his role among aliens and his role among his own lost people. The failure of John is the failure of religion, and John's death is the best argument for Mond's thesis about the absence of God.

In this chapter, finally, the animal of John's dream is revealed — the eagle. Now the figure of the eagle and the skeleton in the rocks on the mesa becomes clear. As Bernard and Lenina climbed up to the foreign mesa's flat top, they caught a glimpse of the future — in the eagle whose proximity is equivalent to John's, and in the bones, which represent John's meaningless death, accomplished at Surrey.

Where the mesa earlier was described as if it were a ship, now John lives in a lighthouse, which gives navigation an aid. Huxley has carefully related the ritual of sacrifice in the Kiva to the orgy and suicide in Surrey. The symbol most emphatically relating the events is the whip, but many other details suggest a close relation between these events.

One abiding irony in the final chapter is Lenina's presence both in the Savage's mind and in her physical being. It is her memory that makes the Savage indulge in his purification in front of Bonaparte's hidden cameras, and it is her presence that makes him rush headlong in madness to use the whip on her and then on himself. To the end he cannot acknowledge the sexual impulse in himself, just as the inhabitants of the Brave New World cannot acknowledge the need for guilt, pain, and God in themselves.

Darwin Bonaparte's name is playful and serious at the same time. Charles Darwin, the great naturalist, first made the case for evolution and postulated that only the fit survive. Bonaparte, the great French general and dictator, could not be stopped in his conquests. The filmmaker, therefore, is an irrepressible seeker after the natural processes, whose images he records for popular amusement. One possible model for Bonaparte is the American filmmaker Robert Flaherty, whose *Nanook of the North*, about an Eskimo family, was a European sensation.

Brave New World

FOREWORD

Summary

Aldous Huxley, speaking in his own voice as opposed to his fictional voice, fifteen years after the publication of *Brave New World*, tells about some of the shortcomings he has discerned in this novel. He has decided against rewriting the work because, in correcting its imperfections, he might have altered many of the features that make it great.

Huxley focuses on the limited choices he set up for the Savage — insane living in a Utopia, or an abnormal existence in the Indian village. He relates that, at the time he was composing the novel, he thought that man was given free will only to choose between equally dehumanizing paths. Further, he admits that the Savage's rationality and reliance on Shakespeare now seem less probable than his despair, self-mutilation and suicide.

Now, in the Foreword, Huxley not only considers sanity to be possible for man but laments that there cannot be more of it. With his characteristic irony, he says he would erect a monument to the world's so-called educators in the ruins of one of the war's bombed-out cities.

If he were to rewrite the book, he would offer his Savage a third alternative — refuge among a community of exiles and refugees from the Brave New World, within the borders of the Reservation. In this third region, economics, politics, religion, and the prevailing philosophy of man would all contribute to man's Final End, or fulfillment. From this community the Savage would proceed to Utopia. This rewriting would give the book "a philosophical completeness."

Looking back to 1931, the year of publication of *Brave New World*, Huxley looks for signs that his predictions about the direction of society were accurate. The first defect in his prophecy is that it makes no mention of nuclear weapons or nuclear energy. Yet Huxley defends his work on the grounds that its theme is the advancement of science "as it affects human beings," the particulars of technological change not being as important as its general relation to life.

As awesome as atomic power seems (this 1946 Foreword came just a year after the first atomic bombs were dropped on

68

Hiroshima and Nagasaki), Huxley sees a greater revolution in the "souls and flesh of human beings." Though not as truly insane as a figure like the notorious Marquis de Sade, the governors of the Brave New World carry out the true revolution of controlling the minds of people in the name of social stability.

Huxley sees that the first phase of what he calls "the penultimate revolution" is nationalistic radicalism, where compromise is impossible and people are hurrying to rush into the confines of narrow dogmatism. He sees that the use of atomic weapons may have taught men to be cautious about the way they wage war. The atomic scientists wil pave the way for mankind and centralized totalitarian governments will force humans to conform. Huxley sees no contemporary movement towards decentralization to counter the menacing growth of totalitarianism.

Huxley argues against the excesses of Nazism by accusing it of inefficiency. In the ideal totalitarian state no force would be necessary because its slaves would love their servitude. The propagandists, editors, and teachers are very inefficient now, but governments will need to study the means of enslavement carefully, to do the job well. Huxley then lists a few necessary developments for the new slave-state: an improved technique of suggestion, a "science of human differences," a substitute for the usual drugs and intoxicants, and a foolproof method of standardizing human beings. Some of the techniques forecast in *Brave New World* will be possible, he says, within three or four generations. The prophecy of sexual freedom is already on its way to fulfillment.

At the time of writing the novel, Huxley set his action 600 years in the future, but only a few years later, in 1946, he sees that the horrors may be upon us by the end of the century. Unless decentralization and humanistic uses of science take place, only totalitarian states or one totalitarian World State is possible.

Commentary

Huxley's aim in writing the Foreword to *Brave New World* is to state unequivocally that the "Utopia" he envisioned when he conceived the novel is arriving sooner than he expected. He begins and ends his treatise with dilemmas. At the start he tells about the too-narrow field of choice open to the Savage. At the end he warns about the too-narrow field of choice for modern man. His wish to have given the Savage a start in a community of exiles and refugees is in some respects a wish that those people in society who still have a vestige of sanity begin there, too. Huxley makes a pretense of being repentant about what he wrote — and says he would have rewritten the book except that it might lose something in the rewriting. Yet for all his apparent focus on the lack of prophetic insight about nuclear power, he actually sees nuclear power as one mighty force in a technological torrent that will sweep all humankind into bondage.

Huxley's satire at certain points shows through his moral seriousness, but in tone and effect the Foreword is meant to send the reader back to reconsider the novel with a sense of urgency. Although at least one critic has seen in the reference to the fifth Marquess of Lansdowne a touch of the humour of the novel, the anecdote concerning that obscure personage is anything but funny. Consider the following list of names that surround the reference: the Marquis de Sade (from whose name we get *sadism*), Robespierre, Hitler, and Hiroshima. Consider that the reference is buried in a passage that connects the infamous Thirty Years War and the Second World War. Clearly Huxley is very serious and intends his reference to apply to censorship, not the Marquess.

Today Hiroshima may seem as strange and as distant as Magdeburg, and Huxley's concern for history — and how little man has learned from it — outmoded or quaint. In fact, Huxley's command of history and intellectual currents may intimidate students who have been taught to disregard memory and to embrace the new "Utopia" unquestioningly. Huxley's allusions span the world — from oriental Tao to the Manhattan Project (where the first atomic bomb was developed in New Mexico) — and some of his allusions, commonplace in his day, have lost much of their immediacy. How many people know that Winston Churchill, the great British statesman, first used the term "iron curtain." Does the term have the menacing overtones today that it did in Huxley's time?

From one point of view, Huxley seems to be reacting to the abuses of the Hitlerian movement in Germany, but that viewpoint is very restrictive. Huxley sees the Nazi movement as horrifying, but less efficient and dehumanizing than the refined governmental control of the future. Huxley relies substantially on one axiom of technocracy: "in an age of advanced technology, inefficiency is the sin against the Holy Ghost." He does not mean to place his argument in Christian terms, but to suggest that the greatest sin of all (from which there can be no retreat to salvation) in the technological state is inefficiency. His argument about the future shape of society depends ultimately on his inherent distrust of efficiency as a criterion of human value. Brute force is inefficient; beloved servitude is completely efficient. Both dehumanize, but the latter is the worst path — and that is the path of the future.

Huxley has almost complete disgust for the so-called educators of modern times. His Latin inscription in memory of the world's educators is to be placed on a monument in a city victimized by the worst of war's ravages. The Jesuits, whom many consider to be the most effective educators in the world, could not stifle a renegade like Voltaire (the 18th-century French philosopher). The role of education seems to have passed from the classroom to the government. Government will dictate the nature of happiness and the means of achieving it. It is curious, then, that educators continue to use *Brave New World* in their classrooms. At the same time that he rails at educators, Huxley appeals to educated people, who will read beyond his particular allusions to his dire warning. The jocularly illiterate saying at the end of the Foreword, "You pays your money and you takes your choice," is meant to separate the people who can see that they have a way out of the dilemma from the people who are powerless to escape. It draws the line along old-school educational lines: those who can read, and understand what they read, may find a refuge. For the others, it is too late.

If Huxley sees hope for mankind, where does he locate that hope? Clearly the Savage is in some respects to be equated with the reader who enters the novel for the first time. In some respects, the book whose title suggests that it is the Utopia of the future, is the alternative — or at least a starting place. Huxley would like to be able to rewrite his prophecy — to give the Savage a more reasonable starting place — but does not. Could this mean that Huxley is not as positive about the direction of history as he would like to be? Does this mean that Huxley really lacks hope for a way out for mankind? Or is he asking that we Savages and exiles, who have formed a community apart, see ourselves clearly for what we are? In this framework the true educators would be meeting the Savage halfway, on the border between the Reservation and the Brave New World.

The reference to Shakespeare is intended to emphasize, not diminish, the importance of that writer in *Brave New World*. It was (and is) a commonplace among humanists that Shakespeare comes closer than any other English writer to encompassing all the possibilities of humankind. The Savage could not have learned everything from his reading of Shakespeare's plays alone, just as the book's title cannot give the full meaning of the book. Yet the banning of Shakespeare is, in humanistic terms, the banning of humankind. And in his isolation on the Reservation, the Savage could have no better guide to the possibilities that no longer seem to exist in the world order. By stating that Shakespeare is insufficient to explain the Savage's knowledge, Huxley emphasizes the role of a *community* in nurturing the real savages who must deal with the world he foresees.

Perhaps Huxley overemphasizes atomics in his Foreword. Now that nuclear power is suspect, and now that SALT (Strategic Arms Limitation Talks) have once again attempted to define the postures of the Superpowers on atomic weapons, Huxley's use of atomics may seem outdated. The limits of atomics are everywhere apparent. Yet Huxley himself warns against the particulars of his pronouncements. It is the general attitudes in a technologically advanced culture that frighten him. Atomic bombs have not deterred man from waging war. There are no atomic-powered helicopters — yet. But if a Manhattan Project were designed to define human happiness once and for all and dictate the refined means by which it may be achieved, a far graver danger to mankind would exist than that of annihilation. For Huxley, the destruction of the world by atomic weapons is not as evil as the destruction of the human spirit by willful enslavement.

Huxley's emphasis on the sexual revolution as taking place much more rapidly than he had thought it would may seem to be old news, now that the Pill is old news. Yet sexuality plays a major role in the novel, and serves there, as in the Foreword, as a symbol of lost values in culture. His iron law of sexuality is as follows: "As political and economic freedom diminishes, sexual freedom tends compensatingly to increase." Huxley is not writing about women's liberation, and, though he can be accused of being sexist in his novels, is not advocating such an abnormal view of sexuality as the Savage has. Those who consider Huxley to be an old-school moralist probably ought to ask themselves how much a product of his prophecy they already are.

Huxley's moral tone is severe, and his answers to the world's ills vague — what is man's Final End if the Greatest Happiness principle is to be secondary to it? More important than the specific remedies for Huxley are the specific steps the opposition must take to impose its will on mankind. This is curious, because Huxley outlines a battle plan for the enemy that is very explicit — including the drug to be used for conditioning. The reader must decide for himself or herself just how prophetic this four-step plan is. Genetic engineering, propaganda and market research, and a refined system of excluding or discouraging "round pegs in square holes" in all sectors of society may yet become more refined, and may indeed already be more refined than many people know.

The Foreword takes *Brave New World* seriously as a moral and prophetic work. Yet the novel stands apart from the treatise that was written later to introduce it. Huxley himself admits that to change the novel could ruin it, however imperfect some parts of it seem in retrospect. The Foreword and *Brave New World Revisited* indicate that behind the mask of the playful satirist of the novel lay an earnest moralist trying to make a statement to all of mankind. The Foreword serves to correct the impression that the novel itself is a frivolous game, meant for an audience of the early nineteen-thirties only. Huxley was a humanist warning mankind against the coming age of the social sciences, sociology, psychology, economics, and so forth, and the hard sciences with their new directions. He is eloquent when he expresses himself in literary form, but less eloquent than others when he tries more direct statements, such as the essay form.

Huxley's courage in reintroducing his work in 1946 and again in 1958 needs some comment. The original work was daring enough, created as it was during the repressive early years of the Great Depression. Yet Huxley reintroduced the work after the devastation of Hiroshima and then after the repressive fifties. Each time Huxley was making a political statement that involved some degree of risk. Ironically, the literary statement is equally useful to the friends and foes of humanity. Consider how, after reading the book, you or your classmates begin to see other people as Gammas or Epsilon-Minuses or to long for *soma*. Less palatable is the dark side of the new world, possibly because many are now thoroughly under its sway.

Brave New World Revisited
Critical Analysis

CHAPTER 1

Overpopulation

Summary

Huxley notes that the prophecies he made in 1931, when he wrote the novel, are coming true much sooner than he expected they would. Freedom is everywhere in danger, even in the West.

George Orwell's *1984* seemed to be more accurate as a prediction of world movements in 1948, but now *Brave New World* seems to be a picture of the way history is moving, because human beings seem to react better to a system of rewards than a system of constraints. Reinforcement of desirable behaviour and scientific manipulation will be more effective than the kind of terrorism exercised in Russia by Stalin. The world will be nightmarish, but not along lines described by Orwell.

Impersonal forces such as the birth rate are making the Brave New World evolve much more rapidly than it would otherwise. Birth control is difficult, and population is advancing at an alarming rate. In the novel an optimum number of people had been arrived at and the world's population was stabilized at that level. Rather than advancing into a Space Age after Sputnik in 1957, the world is advancing into the Age of Over-population. This one great problem will eclipse all others and make totalitarianism inevitable.

Huxley relies on the book *The Next Hundred Years* to demonstrate how dire the situation will become in the poor nations of the earth. Worsening economic conditions will require increasing government measures and controls. Because the underdeveloped nations do not have a tradition of democratic rule, they are easy prey for Communist rule and in twenty years most probably will be under Communist control. Dictatorial control of underdeveloped nations might choke off the flow of raw materials to industrialized nations and put them in a bad way. America is not immune to this problem, but overpopulation will not become critical until the twenty-first century. Militarism is the great danger there.

A permanent state of world crisis will make dictatorship of Communism almost inevitable.

Commentary

The comparison between *1984* and *Brave New World* in Huxley's mind is that between repressive dictatorial control through punishment and extermination *and* a somewhat easier path of reinforcement of natural inclinations. Joseph Stalin's repressive tactics were a matter of fact, as well as legend, and the Communist threat was very real.

Huxley's point about population is simple — food supplies cannot grow as fast as people can, and population growth in underdeveloped countries will jeopardize the world order. Although many means of birth control are available today, the problem of overpopulation still remains difficult and largely unsolved.

CHAPTER 2

Quantity, Quality, Morality

Summary

Huxley says that the breeding program in the novel involved a careful balance of kinds of beings produced — so many Alphas, so many by the Bokanovsky Process, and so on. The historical reality is a tendency towards greater numbers of "biologically poorer quality," both in health and intelligence.

Individual liberty and democratic government are in danger because of the lower IQ's and declining physical vigour. Medical advances have left overcrowding and malnutrition in their wake. And the ostensibly noble desire to let all beings, however deformed, survive will result in "the progressive contamination of the genetic pool."

Commentary

The quality as well as the quantity of people is threatening the political institutions that will allow for individual freedom. Huxley states that mankind is on the "horns of an ethical dilemma" but does not show how we can get off them. If we should kill off or let die the deformed, we are cruel and inhuman. But if we should let the deformed live, we are endangering humanity.

CHAPTER 3

Over-Organization

Summary

Mankind pays a price for technological advances. A Power Elite controls Big Business and the minds of most people. Modern technology has led to the concentration of power. Huxley quotes Erich Fromm, the psychologist, in showing the bad effects of making humans into automatons. Mankind, according to Fromm, is sick. Society is abnormal, forcing humans into inhuman uniformity and destroying individuality.

Mankind desires order, but the Will to Order operating on politics or economics is dangerous to our freedom. Totalitarianism and machine-like men are the fruits of this reduction to uniformity. Huxley would like for society to achieve a balance between uncaring and control.

Individuals have become functions without ultimate meaning in modern society. Like social insects in some respects, humans are too concerned with organization for its own sake. As in William Whyte's *The Organization Man*, people are everywhere subordinating themselves by conforming. Loyalty to the group and wanting to belong are qualities valued in the new Social Ethic. Even sexuality must be subordinated to work.

Huxley contrasts the sexual repression of Orwell's world in *1984* with the sexual freedom of his Brave New World. Pain is the substitute for power in Orwell; in Huxley, pleasure is the stifler of emotional tension.

Social organization is not an end in itself but a means of promoting the good of individuals. Under Hitler and Stalin, violence was the means of social control, but in the future a more subtle social engineering will prevail. The Ph.D.'s of sociology would like to think that no higher authority than themselves is necessary, but Huxley sees that their theories are erroneous. He distrusts those romantically inclined theorists who envision a new medievalism as a perfect society.

Commentary

The enemies of individualism are the sociologists who think they are tomorrow's gods. Huxley warns us against movements already well under way that would enslave the human spirit by enticement to conform. He uses the "bed of Procrustes" as a symbol of how social engineering works. Procrustes was a Greek outlaw who placed his victims on a bed. If the victims were too short for the bed, he stretched their bodies to fit it. If they were too tall for the bed, he cut off enough of them so that they fit it. Sociological systems can never be perfect, and the more rigidly they are defined and enforced, the more inhuman they become.

CHAPTER 4
Propaganda in a Democratic Society

Summary

Quoting Thomas Jefferson, Huxley maintains that most people can probably be trusted with the "direction of their own destinies." Propaganda can be rational and human or passionate and bestial. Reason does not answer every human situation, but it is a good place to start. Jefferson and John Stuart Mill believed in a literate, thinking populace.

The press can be used effectively or abused disgracefully. Censorship is a fact of state policy in the East. It is done by subtle economic control in the West. The concentration of power in the press to a few people has created what Jefferson could not have envisioned — a promulgation not of true or false news but of unreal or irrelevant distractions. Even ancient Rome could not match modern society for the numbers and kinds of mindless distractions. People in democratic societies who spend most of their time in frivolous pleasure will not be able to ward off the devices of those who would control them.

Modern dictators rely on three techniques for their propaganda: repetition, suppression, and rationalization. As the details of technical engineering become more refined, there will be a melding of these methods with the pleasurable distractions, to produce perfect control.

Commentary

Huxley feels that the best avenue for subversion of modern man is through his instinct for pleasure. A man who sits down to read a newspaper for entertainment is most likely to be manipulated by the social engineers of the future. Freedom of the press, always part of democratic government, has been undermined by the way that newspapers are owned and controlled. All of the media have swelled to a vast network of stimuli that surrounds man with propaganda. Huxley foresaw the intense and detailed research that would go into this area, and although he saw a connection between corporate control and desired effects, he did not describe in any detail how this process would work. Even today the process is so complex, subtle, and deeply entrenched that the threads of control are almost impossible to unravel. The best contemporary "emotional engineers" who are permitted to work through the commanding media, may not be entirely aware of why they do what they do, or for whom.

CHAPTER 5
Propaganda under a Dictatorship

Summary

Huxley quotes Albert Speer, who worked for Hitler, on the technical perfection of propaganda in the Third Reich. Although his novel was written before Hitler's rise to power, Huxley maintains that it prophesied a time after the Hitlerian period, with procedures much more advanced than those used by Hitler. Already Chinese and Russian techniques aim well down into the lower leadership to brainwash and control. A plethora of new media give the dictator far greater range of expression.

Hitler's writings contained lucid and true statements about the psychology of his people, especially on crowds and propaganda. He defined a leader as the person able to move the masses. The masses, he thought, were utterly contemptible, and the downtrodden lower middle class, when grouped in great numbers, lost both reason and morality. Hitler knew how to use "herd-poison," the hidden forces lurking in the minds of his people.

Intellectuals, Huxley thinks, are less susceptible to propaganda than the majority of the populace. Hitler thought that intellectuals could not make history. Stereotyped formulas, not reasoned arguments, make people do things, because such formulas arrest doubt. Subhuman mindlessness is the fodder on which the demagogue feeds. Yet how can human individuality assert itself? Huxley has no answer.

Commentary

The terrifying success of Hitler in unifying the German masses is explored in Hitler's own writings and in what others, chiefly Speer and Rauschning, wrote or said about the Hitlerian regime. Huxley would like to think that the world has moved beyond Hitler, and that no man could do now what Hitler did in Hitler's way. Huxley's belief in evolution gives him this conviction. Man must have improved somehow; leadership must have refined its techniques. Huxley might be wrong, for by his own quotations, he seems to imply that Hitler is still a future possibility as well as a buried threat.

Huxley's belief in the intelligentsia may also be a blind spot. Jefferson did not envision an intelligentsia class, but rational men living in a rational society. Huxley does not clarify whom he means by the "intelligentisia," except that they are indecisive because overly critical. Hitler clearly despised the intelligentsia, as did the lower middle class that gave him his power. But Huxley comes perilously close to equating the intelligentsia as the defenders — the only defenders — of human individuality. Since he has excluded sociologists from this group of defenders of freedom, he presumably limits his Jeffersonians to the humanists — those who read and interpret what they read critically. He fears that these people, whoever they are, have little time to speak out and to find an answer.

In one sense the structure of this chapter is that of a trap. At first Hitler is the dead tyrant. Then he becomes a shrewd politician. Finally he becomes a kind of model for the even more capable tyrant(s) who are to come. The reference to Albert Speer is perhaps not as intelligible today as at the time of Huxley's writing. Speer was the most rational and capable of Hitler's ministers. He was the German whom Churchill feared most, because he organized what he controlled like a modern technocrat, with breathtaking efficiency. He was also the most noble spokesman for the Third Reich at the war trials after World War II. His memoirs are well worth reading, though Huxley did not have them when he wrote.

Hermann Rauschning wrote of Hitler's admiration for the Jesuits' abilities at social engineering. Huxley uses Rauschning's remarks to contrast a supposedly godly framework with a supposedly secular one.

CHAPTER 6

The Arts of Selling

Summary

Huxley's view of the new Mr. Hyde is a person with a Ph.D in psychology and an M.A. in the social sciences, preying on the non-rational impulses of mankind for devious purposes. Huxley agrees that commercial propaganda, or selling, is necessary in a capitalist society, but selling propaganda of Hitler's sort is a different matter. Rational propaganda depends on an understanding of the symbols used. Irrational propaganda depends on the symbols not being understood.

Cosmetics are sold because women want to be attractive. Art has for centuries been used to promote religious or political objectives, but the advertising artist does not aim to have his work stand out in time as a masterwork — he wants it to captivate the majority. In the use of music in advertising, sound and conditioned response are wedded, and in the hands of the arch-propagandists, music can make even evil ideas acceptable.

The educational system itself is a main conduit for propaganda. But even the unschooled can be reached by the mass media. Children are particularly susceptible to persuasion. The propagandists' dream is the implantation of trigger words that will later yield the required response without delay. Because of their size, democracies are threatened through the manipulation of multitudes from birth. Political merchandisers market politicians by the same means that they market anything else. Trigger words and images play upon deep fears and hopes. Rationality is excluded from the process. Now the candidate is the entertainer, or even the deodorant. Truth is excluded because it has little to do with marketing.

Commentary

Huxley uses this chapter to draw the reader's attention to ideas presented in Vance Packard's *The Hidden Persuaders*, which every person interested in freedom should read and understand. The techniques of selling are so subtle, refined and effective that they can be used to sell anything the Power Elite wishes. Huxley's enumeration of examples from contemporary advertising do not seem very illuminating, but they combine to warn about the way the experts can manipulate the masses to do their bidding.

Huxley uses the Dr. Jekyll-Mr. Hyde story to distinguish good (rational) from bad (irrational) advertising. It can be used well or abused, and who is to say when it is being used properly?

One aspect of the problem not anticipated by Huxley is the

tendency of humans to disregard a danger once it has been articulated. Huxley does imply that the methods are so fully a part of culture now that truth may not be possible within the framework.

CHAPTER 7

Brainwashing

Summary

Huxley writes that now he turns from mass manipulation to the manipulation of individuals. He turns to the Russian psychologist Ivan Pavlov's experiments with animals, particularly dogs. Stress resistance varies in dogs, but stress, continuously applied, will finally break any dog. The experiments with dogs were verified as applying to human beings during World Wars I and II. The only men able to stand up to stress indefinitely were psychotics, those already insane. Torture has long been used as a tool of the ruler, but now refined torture is used. Learning under stress is made a policy of state. Hitler used fatigue to increase suggestibility. John Wesley, the founder of Methodism, used intense, prolonged fear to break down his listeners and win them to salvation.

Huxley writes that "the effectiveness of political and religious propaganda depends upon the methods employed, not upon the doctrines taught." Everyone is potentially convertible to almost anything. The Communists have shown that they are masters of Pavlovian techniques, and that they use them on enemies and friends alike. The Chinese are particularly adept and turn out armies of conditioned revolutionaries, zealous for their cause.

Huxley sees brainwashing, as now practised, as somewhere between the techniques shown in Orwell's *1984* and those in his *Brave New World*. It is part violence and part psychological manipulation. The society of the future will be in two tiers — the guardians and the domesticated animals. If the guardians get out of line, there will be brainwashing or some island exile. Infant conditioning is still far in the future.

Commentary

Huxley traces the most effective teaching or conditioning to that which engages the central nervous system. Pavlov experimented with dogs, and the World Wars demonstrated with people, that stress can be used in mind management. Some day the present methods may seem crude, but now manipulation is balanced between violence and suggestion. Later perhaps people will be managed through subtle words, images, and tones.

Huxley's image of mankind as a vast herd of domesticated animals is a logical outgrowth of his discussion of the similarities of reactions of men and dogs. Huxley cannot refute the experiments and the results deduced from them, so he draws a logical consequence — mankind will ultimately be controlled. The "wildness" that needs taming through advanced methods of brainwashing is an essential ingredient of value in man.

CHAPTER 8

Chemical Persuasion

Summary

As in Chapter 7, Huxley probes the depths of physical psychology. He begins with the origin of *soma*, which was a drug used in religious rites from ancient times. The *soma* of the novel had no side effects, and it was public, not private. The perfect escape, it was also the perfect tool of the dictator. *Soma* was the people's religion.

Huxley tells about the recent interest in brain chemistry and catalogues substances used by man to affect his brain, from opium to coffee, from amphetamines to marihuana, LSD-25, and the like. He states that the ideal stimulant has not yet been discovered, but that a whole array of substitutes for aspects of *soma* are on the market, cheap: tranquillizers, hallucinogens, stimulants.

The dictator could manipulate people to take drugs in sequence to drive their moods this way and that. Tranquillizers are the most effective in lessening people's desire to make trouble. Further, some drugs now available can, like *soma*, be used to reinforce the effects of government propaganda. Other chemicals will become available over the next few years to provide the dictator with a virtual arsenal of chemical weapons. Pharmacology, biochemistry, and neurology are charging forwards, for good or evil.

Commentary

One of the central symbols of *Brave New World* is *soma*, the wonder drug that pacifies the people and gives them a sense of well-being. Although there is no known drug that will do all that *soma* was supposed to do, many drugs approach its effects as a tranquillizer, or as a vision-enhancer, or as a stimulant. Because government and business can exert some control over the regulation of drugs, presumably they could also use drug management to realize political ends, as Huxley suggests.

One aspect of drugs that particularly interests Huxley is their ability to make people susceptible to ideas. *Soma* assisted the world government of the novel to implant propaganda in its people. Sodium pentothal, to a degree, brings individuals to the border between consciousness and subconsciousness — and it is used in the Communist world for political ends.

The last decades have seen a rise in the use of marihuana and LSD, even though these are illegal for general use. They have also seen movements against caffeine and against tobacco. Clearly some substances are more widely used than others, and some substances are more easily regulated. The government and business are still having trouble defining public tastes, and any widespread control of drugs is still distant in time.

CHAPTER 9

Subconscious Persuasion

Summary

Huxley repeats Freud's account of Poetzl's experiments with a device known as a *tachistoscope*, a device that can project an image briefly on a screen. The study of preconscious perception grew out of the observation that subjects dreamed about parts of a projected image that were not immediately recalled. In fact, people seem to record subconsciously a lot more than they consciously can relate. Further, what they record subconsciously does not lie passive but works actively on the mind. Subliminal projection uses this phenomenon by planting sensations in minds that are not aware of the process. Although no conclusive evidence exists to confirm the effectiveness of subliminal projection in practical situations such as buying popcorn, the possibility itself is suggestive.

Experiments have been conducted to discover the conditions under which minds are most susceptible to suggestion. Huxley prophesies whispering machines placed by a dictator at the most likely environments. Yet the use of subliminal messages must include persuasion, and the best form of that is persuasion-by-association. Huxley tells the story of the German advertisers who sold aspirin to Guatemalans by placing the product below the Holy Trinity. He then tells about an experiment at New York University which showed that people could be influenced to interpret an image in different words or ideas are presented with it. Huxley wonders whether power words, projected subliminally, might enhance a film.

Having set the stage, Huxley imagines the political meeting of the future, with the candidate making his speech while a host of subliminal sounds and images reinforce his message. He says that ten or twenty years in the future this may not seem strange. Huxley regrets that he overlooked subliminal projection in writing his book.

Commentary

The knowledge of subliminal projection has now been around for a while, but political meetings are not as Huxley said they would be. Huxley formulates the idea in too mechanical a fashion, and he wholly neglects the power of a word to speak to a host of remembered images. The intuition that subliminal projection might be a powerful propaganda tool is based on the inability of most people to detect the bald device.

CHAPTER 10

Hypnopaedia

Summary

Huxley tells about a penal institution in Tulare County, California, that used hypnopaedic methods to reform convicts, through moral lessons delivered in the deep of night via pillow speakers. This reminds Huxley of Chapter 2 of *Brave New World*, and he warns against the use of this method, irrespective of the message. The guarantees of freedom in a democracy would be violated by condoning hypnopaedia. Huxley suggests that the method be regulated by law.

One problem with defining the effectiveness of sleep-teaching is defining what sleep is, in all its stages. In spite of the inadequacy of experimentation in this field, many uses have been developed, and some seem to work.

Huxley tells about an article by Theodore X. Barber, in which light sleep and deep sleep are distinguished, the former by the presence of alpha waves, as detected by an electroencephalograph. People in light sleep are suggestible, as if they are in a state of hypnosis. Huxley tells about Wetterstrand, who treated children by hypnosis while they were asleep. For Huxley there is enough evidence to suggest that hypnopaedia can work, with a full range of implications for dictatorial control of the people.

Suggestibility varies from person to person. In an experiment at the Massachusetts General Hospital, a large number of patients just out of surgery were divided into groups, one receiving morphine, one water. Fourteen percent of the patients who received only water claimed to have relief whenever they received the injections. Neither sex nor IQ seemed to make a difference — temperament did. In comparison, twenty percent of people hypnotize easily, and one manufacturer of hypnopaedic materials claimed that twenty percent of his customers were enthusiastic about the results. In a democracy a high percentage of suggestibles can mean control, especially for the individual who can make the key suggestions.

After posing the problem, Huxley asks how society can protect itself against those who would use this knowledge against democracy itself.

Commentary

Since Huxley wrote *Revisited*, the study of sleep has raced ahead. Now many levels and kinds of sleep are known, and numerous experiments have been done on subjects to test the limits of hypnopaedia. The legislation that Huxley called for has not been passed.

Huxley finds more evidence in favour of hypnopaedia than of other prophecies he made in his novel, and he demonstrates the widespread applications of the method. Yet personality profiles were in their infancy when Huxley wrote, and a whole science within managerial science has grown up, with centres all around the world for the testing of personality types, on the basis of which people are categorized, hired, fired, promoted, or frozen in place. The relationship of personality profiles to the tendency of hypnopaedic suggestion, or waking suggestibility, is not known.

Huxley's fears about people most susceptible to suggestion are well founded, yet earlier in the work Huxley admitted that anyone can be induced to believe anything under stress.

CHAPTER 11

Education for Freedom

Summary

Huxley's prescription for education is a foundation of facts and values, and the aim of education is to make people free. The biological principle upon which his humanistic education rests is that humans are all different. Huxley disagrees with such noted behaviourist scientists as J.B. Watson and B.F. Skinner, who value individual contributions at zero. Instead, he reminds his readers of the thoughts of William James, who wrote that great men had a profound effect on history. Skinner and others like him take too narrow a view. On the other hand, Bertrand Russell considers important individuals to be one of the three forces that change history. Unfortunately for mankind, people who think like the behaviourists have incorporated their thinking in nearly every major institution in society, including education.

Huxley sees the prevailing perspective as similar to the one that produced witch hunts, Communism, and the Nazi ethic, more appropriate to insects than to humans. Since Big Business and Big Government cannot control mankind's genetic uniformity — yet — they will work very hard to impose social and cultural uniformity on everyone. To avoid the tyranny that seems inevitable, Huxley urges education for freedom now.

Huxley's program would include "the facts of individual diversity and genetic uniqueness and the values of freedom, tolerance, and mutual charity." The forces of evil propaganda must be combatted by a critical study of language, which would include a full study of the devices that are used against freedom.

Huxley points out the problem with his program in the need for governments to use propaganda specifically to protect freedom, as when the USA used it against the Nazis. Ironically, an outcry against the Institute for Propaganda Analysis was mounted by educators, military officials, clergy, and advertising experts. Huxley admits that making people as a whole too critical may lead to cynicism and even subversion. He suggests finding a happy medium between making people willing to help society and yet making them aware of the wiles of mind-manipulators.

Above all, values need to be taught — individual freedom, charity and compassion, and intelligence. With these values, humans should be able to pierce through the veil of propaganda, and they should be able to remain free.

Commentary

The arguments Huxley mounts against the biological determinists may seem protracted and unnecessary, but in them he is attacking the same kinds of social scientists he wrote of earlier in this work — those who would enslave society by social and managerial engineering. Skinner was particularly formidable. As the leading behaviourist, he was profoundly influential. Those who wish to control mankind want to believe that all people are easily categorized and easily manipulated, that all are essentially the same, and that individuals are not very important in the historical process. Huxley noticed that the system of education was already deeply imbued with behaviourist ideas, and that the study of language arts was neglected. In *Brave New World*, except for technical manuals, no person has free access to books except the World Controller.

Huxley's values are conventional — freedom, charity, and intelligence — but when he backtracks to suggest that caution must be exerted in the teaching of language, or when he implies that perhaps not everyone should be given the same training in anti-propaganda language skills, he undoes some good work. Huxley is a humanist, and he believes that language and literature can free mankind. As a humanist, he finds himself under attack by the social scientists, but he cannot wholly dismiss their arguments. Fortunately he has good thinkers from their camp on his side. William James and Bertrand Russell are powerful allies.

Huxley's biggest problem may be his greatest strength. He does not conceive of the human social order as ideally termite-like, and he does believe in individuals having a role in history. Yet he does not want to see demagogues and charlatans abusing mankind. He does not want to create an anarchy of super-critical individuals, but he does not want to create a nation of sheep. In short, he wants to walk the middle way between extremes. He wants to place value on genetic differences and on environmental differences, and to teach respect for human differences. At the same time he would like to teach respect for the integrity of the social order, which would allow freedom to be exercised, without making it a dictatorship masquerading as a free society.

Right from the outset Huxley makes clear his intolerance of those who would oppose his system: "Education . . . must go on to develop appropriate techniques . . . for combating those who, for whatsoever reason, choose to ignore the facts or deny the values." And Huxley's regard for tradition comes out clearly at the end: people "should be taught enough about propaganda analysis to preserve them from an uncritical belief in sheer nonsense, but not so much as to make them reject outright the not always rational outpourings of the well-meaning guardians of tradition." Huxley's guarantee that his own system will not become another form of tyranny is the foundation of values under it

CHAPTER 12
What Can Be Done?

Summary
Huxley maintains that freedom is threatened by factors that are demographic, social, political, and psychological. People must be educated for freedom now. He highlights social organization for freedom, birth control for freedom, and legislation for freedom.

Huxley refers to English law and applauds the writ of *habeas corpus*, but he says there will never be a writ that can demand the presence of a person's mind. Huxley would see a law against sleep-teaching, one against subliminal projection, one against excessive spending in a political campaign. Even with such laws, society is not out of danger. Overpopulation and overorganization will create out of the old political system "a new kind of non-violent totalitarianism."

To deal with overpopulation, the birth rate must be reduced so that it does not exceed the death rate, and natural resources managed to increase food and fuel. In the absence of a Pill for birth control, some way must be found to reduce the birth rate — and problems of all sorts are involved here. As for educating the agricultural poor, what will be the effects? And how soon can the industrial and social potential of under-developed nations be enhanced? Both food and raw materials will be in short supply by the end of the century.

To protect democracy, Huxley recommends that property be distributed as widely as possible and that governments be restructured in smaller units, with more direct input from citizens than now. The small community should be revived, inside and outside the metropolis. This idea is not new, and Huxley gives his antecedents, as well as literary and experimental examples of the small society at work. But even though the idea has been widely thought upon, the disease of overorganization continues.

Huxley asks a crucial question: does mankind really want to solve the problems he poses? In America the youth have no faith in democracy, do not object to censorship, and would not mind being ruled by an oligarchy of experts. He quotes from the interview between Alyosha Karamazov and the Grand Inquisitor in Dostoevsky's *Brothers Karamazov*: "nothing has ever been more insupportable for a man or a human society than freedom." The urge towards freedom diminishes as long as people are well fed, but if conditions change, they will rise up in their chains. Yet, Huxley maintains, "there seems to be no good reason why a thoroughly scientific dictatorship should ever be overthrown."

In the face of the defeatist or apathetic attitude of youth, Huxley says he still believes in freedom, and those who believe with him have a duty to resist the forces that would defeat it.

Commentary

Huxley did not know that the Pill would become an actuality, though it was under consideration in his time. But the Pill has not solved the problem of world population. The problems of scarcity of food and resources also remain. Perhaps the greatest problem articulated by Huxley, although his optimism prohibited him from giving it full emphasis, is the attitude of the youth of America towards freedom. For if youth does not value freedom, the future will surely be slavery. And not only do the young people fail to see the value of freedom, they also wish for some form of benign totalitarian control. Overpopulation and overorganization may be inevitable even if people rise to the banner of freedom now, but the freedom fighters are few and time is short.

Huxley's choice of Dostoevsky for his final literary allusion is significant, because the interview between Alyosha and the Inquisitor (which no literate person should miss reading in its entirety!) is very similar to the interchange between the Savage and the World Controller in *Brave New World*. The World Controller, in spite of his name (*Mustapha* Kemal plus Sir Alfred *Mond*), is a direct descendant of the Inquisitor, working in an order more carefully arranged because science informs every part of it. The Savage's solitude is a last bid for freedom in a world that finally will not allow it. Mond, like the Inquisitor, seems to sense the special nature of his captive, but the Savage is still part of the "experiment" when he leaves the Controller's presence, while Alyosha is just free.

The dodo, now extinct, is what mankind will become if we do not think about freedom now. We will no longer be able to fly, though we may wish to fly to escape our captors later. Man, Huxley says, will sacrifice his wings of freedom to become flightless like the dodo, and regret the act later, when the game is up.

Huxley's aim is not to present a program which, if followed, will solve the problems he presents. In fact, his statement of the problems is vague and incomplete. What Huxley wants to do is sound the alarm for freedom. His last essay is like the conclusion of a sermon.

Character Sketches *(Brave New World)*

Bernard Marx

Glum, given to melancholy, physically deformed, Marx is a typical Huxleyan anti-hero — full of ideas but sterile when it comes to action. He is one we clearly do not wish to identify with. His inner conflicts make him suffer throughout the length of the novel and lose in the end — both his struggle and himself. Small and dark, when he should be tall and fair like the Alpha-plus that he is, a social outcast, he is at heart an opportunist who greedily seizes and savors the little power he can wheedle as John's mentor. Unlike Watson, his rancorous nonconformity comes from his bitterness toward the state and its citizens rather than from ideals and deep conviction. His loneliness makes him resent even the friendliness of Watson and John.

Like all anti-heroes, Bernard is a misfit, a self-conscious rebel with all sorts of faults: he is characterized by his failure to achieve status and his disdain for the social mores. Despite his superior Alpha-plus mind, Bernard suffers from an inferiority complex. He is a vain-glorious boaster who details greatly inflated accounts of his deeds to his only real friend, Helmholtz Watson. He is also a coward who indulges in outbursts of the most abject self-pity. Disgusted with hedonism and yearning for love, Bernard spends most of his time by himself. He symbolizes the conflict between rebelliousness and a sense of its futility. Gyrating in the realm of rebellion, he is not able to project his thought processes, willingly or unwillingly, into that rarified atmosphere of "reasoned-out ideas" which usually stimulate creative revolt.

At times Bernard is repulsive. When he finally achieves social status he does everything which, previously, he has mocked and disdained — partly because he could not attain the required status. He is completely unable to cope with success, going to self-satisfied and selfish extremes when he finally does achieve what he might term as success.

Bernard is a talker but not a doer. When arrested with John and Watson, he first tries to escape and then swears he had nothing to do with the other two. When he learns that he is to be exiled, he creates such a scene that he has to be subdued by soma. But just before he leaves with Watson, he finally accepts his fate and apologizes to John for his conduct.

John (the Savage)

Perhaps he is the most enigmatic character in the story. Attractive and fair, wholesomely educated, often moved to tears, it is not easy to understand the roof of his guilt complex and his profound need for suffering. John's self-condemnation may be grounded in the facts of his birth, which was the principal reason for the enforced exile of his mother from Utopia. He looks forward with great eagerness to being transported to Utopia where he anticipates exploring to its depths a world such as the one opened for him by Shakespeare. He is a symbol of the artist striving for ecstasy.

John, the Noble Savage, also symbolizes the classical hero — the lone wolf who combines the mythical virtues of integrity, unity, and a belief in personal values. To him, personal liberty is absolutely essential to human dignity and happiness. In his actions and ideals he represents Wordsworth's famous dictum:

We must be free or die, who speak the tongue
That Shakespeare spake; the faith and morals hold
Which Milton held.

Structurally speaking, the introduction of John, the eternal innocent, to a completely foreign environment, is a traditional device. John is a moralist who acts as a touchstone in exposing the faults of the other characters and their society. The eternal innocent must learn to be like everybody else or perish.

John also symbolizes the struggle to become a whole or natural man who, though he yearns to be part of the world, can be at home neither in the primitive Reservation, nor in a wholly mechanized society. The term, 'Savage,' is applied to John by the brave new world inhabitants who equate it with primitivism: to a mechanized world, his naturalness seems primitive. But primitive man and natural man are not synonymous. The primitive man is the raw material, while the natural man is the finished product in Lawrence's sense of the term.

John is Huxley's second portrait of D.H. Lawrence. (The first was that of Mark Rampion in *Point Counter Point*.) Like Lawrence, John is a hopeful specimen who cannot succeed in his environment. Heroism is impossible under conditions of perfect adaptation. In his rejection of the mechanistically determined *Brave New World*, John reacts just as Lawrence did to a sterile London society that was unable to feel or sympathize.

In addition, John symbolizes Huxley's principle of non-attachment in a super-attached society. When he cannot convince Mustapha Mond, he seeks escape by non-attachment to bodily sensations and lusts. He equates salvation, deliverance and enlightenment with self-obliteration.

But John is not a whole man: he is struggling towards that goal. Neither of the two social orders with which he has been involved will allow him to attain this. In the Savage Reservation he is, as an outsider, forcibly prevented from participating in the manhood rites. His relationship with his mother, Linda, has always been ambivalent. Since she was conditioned against motherhood, she alternately accepts and rejects her son. On the other hand, the sternly idealistic boy is filled with disgust and hatred for his mother's numerous lovers. He dramatizes repressions and half-hidden wants with which he cannot cope.

Symbolically, John also represents the theme of love versus sex in his relationship with Lenina. She tries to arouse him with false allure which she believes is real sexual freedom. But in his inflexible belief in the nature of love, John can only repulse her. He tries to sublimate his sensual feelings, which he regards as impure, through self-inflicted beatings and other punishments. Thus, the Savage also symbolizes the "ultimate sacrifice." The bloody self-flagellation is his way of trying to redeem his spirit and expiate the sins of a world neither good, nor brave, nor beautiful. This sacrificial theme is introduced with John when we first meet him on the Savage Reservation and continues throughout the book.

Mustapha Mond

His fordship, Mustapha Mond, is the London Resident Controller for Western Europe and one of the Ten World Controllers. Of middle height, the black-haired Mond has a hooked nose, full red lips and very piercing dark eyes. Structurally, his role is to explain the rationale behind the brave new world. Symbolically, Mond represents the Huxleyan principle that hedonism must be absolutely rational. He is dark, inscrutable, almost sinister, and is a World Controller in the utmost sense. He would never sully himself with physical violence, nor would he stoop to common invective. He is the diplomat and perfect gentleman, while ruling with an iron hand.

A disenchanted man of the world, Mond rather despises

the characters and society he rules. As a young Alpha-plus with non-conformist ideas, he had had the chance to escape this role by choosing voluntary exile. He had the choice between his own happiness — non-conformity with discomfort — and serving other people's happiness — conformity with comfort: he chose the latter. He knows the establishment of Utopia is irreversible and that it is a closed system which needs little effort to keep it running. In this knowledge alone consists his happiness. As Mond says, "happiness — it's all relative."

He is a beneficent despot whose role is to find exactly the correct proportions of bread and circuses, routines and orgies, to keep the brave new world running. As such, he has sacrificed his spirit. In his discussions with the Noble Savage, Mond reveals that he, too, knows and owns copies of Shakespeare and other works forbidden to everyone else. In his actions, Mond brings to mind the famous passage from Milton's *Areopagitica*: "As good almost kill a man as kill a good book: who kills a man kills a reasonable creature, God's image; but he who destroys a good book kills reason itself, kills the image of God, as it were, in the eye."

Helmholtz Watson

Helmholtz Watson is a superb Alpha-plus who seems well on his way to filling Mond's shoes at the proper time. Extremely handsome and brilliant, he is an Emotional Engineer in the Department of Writing. The only possible criticism against him (by his jealous superiors) is that he is perhaps "a little *too* able." He is Bernard's best friend. Helmholtz symbolizes the predicament of the specialist whose dissatisfaction with the world arises from the prohibition of his freedom of self-expression. By nature, he is a poet but must write propaganda to support the system. After John introduces him to Shakespeare, Watson discerns what true poetry is. Thus, he supports John's ideas. Realizing that suffering and frustration are necessary for creation, he accepts voluntary exile in preference to stability and conformity.

Linda

Linda, John's mother, is a pathetic symbol of the displaced person. Starting out as a perfect Beta-minus, she was utterly incapable of understanding, or in any way adapting herself, to the mores of the Savage Reservation. Twenty-five years before the book opens she had been an attractive blonde and a very adept ("pneumatic") sexual companion. Brought back to her brave new world at the age of forty-four, she is a repulsive specimen of physical decay. Symbolically, she is outwardly decayed in a decadent society where her still beautiful contemporaries are all inwardly decayed.

Linda is unable to make choices. For example, she could have abandoned the infant, John, and returned to London. Despite her conditioning, she has something of a mother-son relationship with John, though a greatly ambivalent one. Once she returns to London, she abandons herself to a permanent soma holiday. To perpetuate his own brand of irony, Huxley, in the death scene has John mourn her state and attempts to assuage her suffering, while she dies amidst her own sexual fantasies involving one of her Reservation lovers.

Lenina Crowne
Lenina is a superb Beta specimen who works as a technician in the Central London Hatchery and Conditioning Centre. She symbolizes the virtuous English girl of her society. Very popular, she has spent a night with almost all the Alpha men she knows. Still, she symbolizes the imperfection of *Brave New World* in stifling feelings of true love. From the very beginning, Lenina exhibits non-conformist tendencies by sleeping only with Henry Foster for an unusually lengthy period of time (actually four months). Although her conditioning has made Lenina incapable of understanding her feelings, she loves the Savage as much as she is able to, but cannot understand him.

Tomakin
Tomakin, the London D.H.C. (Director of Hatcheries and Conditioning) is a tall, thin, but upright man with a long chin and rather prominent teeth. He symbolizes the Organization Man, the conforming Manager who unquestioningly accepts and propagates the values of his world. Super-attachment is his key to fulfillment. Anybody who is "different" is either abnormal or deficient. The D.H.C. is a conventional figure of satire who also shows that though the world structure has changed, human nature has not improved: people are still petty, hypocritical, malicious, dishonest, emotionally sterile and quite

capable of revenging themselves on others for their own lapses of accepted "good taste."

Henry Foster

Henry Foster is an up-and-coming Organization Man. An ambitious hustler, he is part and parcel of the system. His main function seems to be as a contrast of contentment from orthodoxy with Bernard's misery from nonconformity.

A ruddy, young Alpha with vivacious blue eyes, he is Lenina's current lover when the book opens. He has more sense, however, than to stick to one girl. Being absolutely on time is one of his main principles. Henry is a junior version of the D.H.C. He is only too happy to poke malicious fun at Bernard because of his height. Just as the D.H.C. abandoned Linda on the Reservation, so Foster treats Lenina. At the book's end he accompanies her to John's hideout. But when the Savage turns on Lenina with his whip, Henry abandons her by making a hasty retreat.

Selected Criticisms

Everyone who has ever read *The Sleeper Wakes* remembers it. It is a vision of a glittering, sinister world in which society has hardened into a caste-system and the workers are permanently enslaved. It is also a world without purpose, in which the upper castes for whom the workers toil are completely soft, cynical and faithless. There is no consciousness of any object in life, nothing corresponding to the fervour of the revolutionary or the religious martyr.

In Aldous Huxley's *Brave New World*, a sort of post-war parody of the Wellsian Utopia, these tendencies are immensely exaggerated. Here the hedonistic principle is pushed to its utmost, the whole world has turned into a Riviera hotel. But though *Brave New World* was a brilliant caricature of the present (the present of 1930), it probably casts no light on the future. No society of that kind would last more than a couple of generations, because a ruling class which thought principally in terms of a 'good time' would soon lose its vitality. A ruling class has got to have a strict morality, a quasi-religious belief in itself, a mystique. . . .

In Huxley's book the problem of 'human nature' is in a sense solved, because it assumes that by pre-natal treatment, drugs and hypnotic suggestion the human organism can be specialised in any way that is desired. A first-rate scientific worker is as easily produced as an Epsilon semi-moron, and in either case the vestiges of primitive instincts, such as maternal feeling or the desire for liberty, are easily dealt with. At the same time no clear reason is given why society should be stratified in the elaborate way that is described. The aim is not economic exploitation, but the desire to bully and dominate does not seem to be a motive either. There is no power hunger, no sadism, no hardness of any kind. Those at the top have no strong motive for staying at the top, and though everyone is happy in a vacuous way, life has become so pointless that it is difficult to believe that such a society could endure.

George Orwell

Aldous Huxley, like George Orwell, W.H. Mallock, G.K. Chesterton and Charles Williams, is a pseudo-novelist; I use the expression not harshly, but merely to describe an author who finds himself using the form of the novel for some alien purpose. Mr. Huxley's purpose is to write tracts. . .

Brave New World is . . . an anti-materialist tract. It is a well-understood convention that the Utopian kind of pseudo-novel, though set in a remote position as to period or place, is always a criticism of the author's own society. *Brave New World* is a criticism of Western society in 1932, as *1984* is of the same society in the closing months of the Second World War; any discussion of such books that sets out to assess their plausibility as *predictions* seem to me hopelessly off-centre. The citizens of the Brave New World are entirely conditioned to a life which ignores the possibility of any values except those of pleasure and material well-being; they live in great physical comfort which is paid for in terms of an appalling spiritual dryness. As a criticism of the more prosperous Western countries in the late 'twenties it could not be bettered; the "prophetic" framework is valuable largely because it allows free play to the author's marvellous wit (the jokes about Ford, etc.).

The thrust against materialism had point in 1932, and has point now; but in the actual future, I doubt if it will have any. People who live very primitive and physically exhausting lives are never materialistic; on the contrary, they are always deeply religious. And it will, of course, be a primitive and laborious life that human beings will live in a hundred years' time and indefinitely thereafter; even if there are no World Wars, the increase of population, coupled with the exhaustion of natural resources, will usher in an era of famine and shortage. Our great-grandchildren will listen open-mouthed to stories of the 1950's, when even quite ordinary people had motor cars of their own, to go more or less where they liked, and could buy petrol without a police permit; people who lived in houses which could be warmed by merely switching on an electric fire, and where hot water gushed out of the taps! I think, in short, that humanity has already reached the most highly urbanized and gadget-ridden state it is ever likely to reach; anyone who wants to know how the peoples of the Western countries will be living in a century's time could find out more from a tour of South-East Asia than anything else: that swarming, half-starved proletariat — *that* is our future, not a world in which ordinary citizens take trips by helicopter from London to New York.

It was the brave *old* world that Mr. Huxley was describing;

the world with a tremendous material ascendancy, whose natural danger was sceptical materialism. In the world we are actually going to inhabit, the dangers will be devil-worship and witch-burning. But this fact does not, of course, diminish the value of Mr. Huxley's works.

John Wain

In thematic terms, *Brave New World* opposes the scientific-industrialist ideal of Mustapha Mond (and, by derivation, of Henry Ford) to the primitivist vitalism of Lawrence, the acceptance of life with all its joys and miseries, as it exists. A decade later Huxley criticized himself for having failed to add a third possibility, that of the decentralized, libertarian society, where industry is minimized and man is liberated to pursue the life of time by the illumination of eternity. Yet it is difficult to see how the novel could have been changed to include this third possibility. The anti-individualist tendencies latent in our society have to be opposed by the poetic primitivism of the savage, who, alone, since he is the only character conscious of the nature of tragedy, can embody the tragic possibilities of man's future.

One is tempted to consider *Brave New World*, because it is a Utopian fantasy, as an exceptional work that stands outside the general pattern of Aldous Huxley's fiction. In reality, its function is to close the sequence of the earlier novels. The central characters belong clearly in the Huxleian succession. Bernard is a latter-day Gumbril who has to inflate himself perpetually in order to feel equal to others, and who can only fulfill himself in exceptional circumstances. Helmholtz is a Calamy, an expert amorist who has lost his taste for sensual delights and longs for something more elevated and intelligent. The savage is a more acceptable vehicle for the Lawrencian viewpoint than the excessively didactic Rampion. And Mustapha Mond, with his orotund delivery, is a Scogan or a Cardan who has at last made good. As for the world of the novel, it is the Bohemia of *Antic Hay* and *Point Counter Point*, carried to its logical end, its pleasures sanctified and its personal irresponsibilities institutionalized so that the freedom of the libertine is revealed as the most insidious of slaveries. There can be no doubt of the continuity between *Brave New World* and the earlier novels. It is the direction of the journey that has changed.

George Woodcock

In his new book (*Brave New World Revisited*) Mr. Huxley surveys the technological advances and political trends of the last thirty years, and considers that, on the available evidence, the future is more likely to resemble his own Brave New World than the world of *1984*. . . . Referring to *1984*, he points out, with some justice, that "recent developments in Russia, and recent advances in science and technology, have robbed Orwell's books of some of its gruesome verisimilitude," and he considers that the further advance of totalitarian rule will be effected less by violence than by the increasing use of propaganda, brain-washing, subliminal persuasion and the various tranquillizing or stimulant drugs. The greater part of the book is taken up with a comparative analysis of these non-violent instruments of power, and the facts which Mr. Huxley has assembled are both fascinating and extremely frightening. He feels, as he says, a good deal less optimistic now than he did in 1932, when Hitler had not yet come to power and Stalinism had hardly got into its stride. . . .

This is a saddening book, not only because of its profound pessimism, but because it invites comparison with the novel to which it is a pendant. In *Brave New World* Mr. Huxley was still writing with much of his original brio, and one misses here, as in all his later work, the gaiety and wit which made his earlier books so enjoyable. Goodness knows, there is little enough nowadays to be gay about, but one notices an increasing tiredness in Mr. Huxley's writing, and a growing habit (always a danger with him) of dropping into literary clichés — e.g., Man's inhumanity to man, Beauty-is-truth-truth-beauty, Theirs not to reason why, etc, etc. Mr. Huxley remains as wise, humane and inexhaustibly intelligent as ever; but he says little or nothing in this book which he has not said, more cogently and more eloquently, before.

Jocelyn Brook

No one can deny the importance of his work to his contemporaries; and the interest which it has roused confirms it. He has succeeded in recording modes of feeling and thinking characteristic of his own generation which have never been described before. He has made his contemporaries more aware of their own responses, moral, amoral, aesthetic and intellectual; their indifference, impatience, obtusity, disappointment, sensibility.

He has diagnosed subtly and mercilessly the diseases of modern self-consciousness, and described the ignobly comic falsifications of emotions which result from them. But this is not for the critic the central fact about him. His distinguishing mark is that he stands out as the most deeply and widely cultured of modern novelists. I am not sure that even in the past one can point to any other writer of fiction who has illumined his picture of life with cross lights drawn from an equal familiarity with contemporary knowledge and theory. George Eliot only comes near to him. . . .

The peculiarity of Mr. Huxley's work is that not only science in all its branches is frequently laid under contribution, but also the history of art, music, poetry, medicine, society and philosophy. What is disconcerting is the contrast between the extraordinary many-coloured richness of the light he pours upon his subjects, and that these subjects are taken from small and often stuffy corners of the big common world of experience. He is the most universal of novelists in his references and one of the most limited in focus. His constant theme is love and sex, and the result of his investigations is dissatisfaction, or more positively disgust.

. . . This preoccupation he shares with his age, which is thinking as hard and confusedly about sex as the one preceding it thought about religion. Hence the peculiar interest of his fiction to his contemporaries. . . .

Clearly there is little that the critic can tell Mr. Aldous Huxley about his work that he does not already know himself. . . Critics must accept him as a writer not "deep" but "wide." They must accept his novels and stories being disquisitions illustrated by characters, since his supreme merit lies in width of reference, and in putting facts in juxtaposition which his omnivorous reading and perpetual reflection have assembled. The deep pleasure in reading Mr. Huxley lies in following the movement of his mind. He is aware also of the irritation produced in some readers by his inevitably discursive methods.

Desmond MacCarthy

Review Questions and Answers

Question 1.

How does Huxley structure the novel so that he is able to parallel life in the *Brave New World* with our life today?

Answer

Huxley uses John as the bridge between the culture on the Reservation and the culture of Utopia. Thus, we hear John uttering platitudes which echo the conventional view of morality amid the splendors made by scientific endeavors and discoveries. However, John is alone and ultimately succumbs to the temptations of the secular world. Thus, the pleasure principle which governs the lives of the other characters envelops John and, in despair, he commits suicide. There is no room for the idealist in the modern world of technology.

Question 2.

How important is the World Controller to the development of the novel and the expression of Huxley's ideas?

Answer

The World Controller is one of the most important characters because he is the most intelligent and the most knowledgeable — he has read and studied many forbidden books. His own unconventionality necessitated a choice between life on an island and life in the World State. Because the Controller has freedom of choice — a freedom which conditioning normally inhibits or destroys — he is one of the few real individuals we meet in this novel.

Question 3.

How does the World Controller aid the development of Huxley's basic thesis?

Answer

In the latter part of the novel the conversation between the Controller and John the Savage is the device Huxley uses to "put across" his own ideas and concerns. When the Controller explains his values and beliefs, his arguments and explanations are clearly and logically presented; his sanity makes the insanity of the Brave New World all the more vivid and frightening. The Controller in many ways represents the intelligent, capable individual who uses his intelligence and capability for unworthy ends.

Question 4.
What is Lenina's importance in the development of the novel?

Answer
Lenina is a fairly important character because she is instrumental in bringing about the suicide of John the Savage, although we cannot in any way blame her. (She is the product of the system, and the system is wrong.) Because she is a beautiful, desirable woman, she personifies for John the conflict between the body and the spirit. In a way, she repeats the conflict he felt regarding his mother — he is at one and the same time attracted and repelled by the object of his affections.

Question 5.
Why is John considered the most important character in the book?

Answer
John is the most important character in the book because he acts as a bridge between the two cultures, and having known both "ways of life" he is able to compare them and comment on them. His beliefs and values are a curious mixture of Christian and heathen, of "Jesus and Pookong," but, most important, he has a strict moral code. His old-fashioned beliefs about God and right and wrong (his beliefs closely duplicate Christian morality), contrast sharply with the values and beliefs of the citizens of the Brave New World. It is this conflict between the two value systems that ultimately brings about his suicide.

Question 6.
What is the significance of the World State's motto?

Answer
The World State's motto emphasizes the importance of the group and the subsequent unimportance of the individual.

Community stresses the importance attached to the individual as a contributor to society. Reference is made to the contribution the individual makes even after death. *Identity* refers to the various classes (castes), their specialized duties, and their distinguishing uniform. In the lower classes, identity was stressed even more since there might well be ninety-six identical twins performing a particular task in a single factory. *Stability* is the key word in the World State. Decanting and conditioning, the abolition of the family, and conformity in thought and action all contribute to a stable society.

Question 7.
What is the significance of Huxley's use of "Ford" as a substitute for "Christ" or "God?"

Answer
In the Brave New World, science and technology have replaced God as a source of value and meaning in life. Because Huxley believed that this shift in emphasis was given great impetus when Henry Ford revolutionized manufacturing with his assemblyline technique, the introduction of the Model-T Ford is used as the opening date of the new era. This change in emphasis is symbolized by the changing of the Christian Cross to the Ford T.

Suggested Study Topics

1. What is Huxley's attitude toward science? How does he contrast it with technology? Do you think such a comparison is common in current literature?

2. Has man *always* written about Utopia? Is there any promise of one being attainable? How is the adjective "utopian" used?

3. What is Huxley's attitude toward the flesh? How is this manifested through the actions of the principal characters in *Brave New World*?

4. The civilization Huxley depicts represents the magnification of negative ideas. This kind of society has often been called a Utopia-in-reverse. What does this mean? Is a Utopia-in-reverse more likely to be realized than a Utopia? How many devices might they share in common. Taken on its own terms, is the brave new world without flaws?

5. *Brave New World* has been described by some as a satire of a "hopelessly drifting age." If so, what does the novel satirize? Try to relate the satirized subject or object with its real-world correlative. Do we find irony in the two works under consideration? Paradox?

6. Mystical religion was one of the preoccupations of Huxley's later life. Is there any evidence of its influence in either of the works discussed?

7. In *Point Counter Point*, Huxley discusses two of his literary notions; "the musicalization of fiction" and "the novel of ideas." What do you suppose he means by these?

8. In his earlier novels, Huxley ridiculed the aristocrats and Bohemians of postwar London, who devoted their existences to social revelry and chit-chat. Show how these same failings in human nature feature in *Brave New World* and *Brave New World Revisited*.

9. In *Brave New World*, what do you think of some of Huxley's devices for mass amusement and control. Describe some. Is there a chance of their invention?

10. How is the principle of mass production applied to biology in this book?

11. Tone of voice is an essential ingredient of style. Discuss Huxley's tone of voice in this book. Is it satire or preaching? Is it prophecy or fantasy?

Bibliography

Atkins, John A. *Aldous Huxley: A Literary Study.* New York: Roy Publishers, 1956.

Bedford, Sybille. *Aldous Huxley: A Biography,* Volume One: 1894-1939, London: Chatto & Windus and Collins, 1973.

Birnbaum, Milton. *Aldous Huxley's Quest for Values.* Knoxville: University of Tennessee Press, 1971.

Bowering, Peter. *Aldous Huxley: A Study of the Major Novels.* London: Athelone Press, 1968.

Brander, Lawrence. *Aldous Huxley: A Critical Study.* Lewisburg: Bucknell University Press, 1970.

Clareson, Thomas D. and Andrews, Carolyn S. *Aldous Huxley: A Bibliography, 1960-1964.* In *Extrapolation 6,* no. 1 (1964/65).

Daiches, David. *The Novel and the Modern World.* Chicago: University of Chicago Press, 1939.

Eschelbach, Claire John and Shober, Joyce Lee (foreword by Aldous Huxley). *Aldous Huxley, A Bibliography: 1916-1959.* Berkeley and Los Angeles: University of California Press, 1961.

Firchow, Peter. *Aldous Huxley: Satirist and Novelist.* Minneapolis: University of Minnesota Press, 1972.

Hillegas, Mark R. *The Future as Nightmare: H.G. Wells and the Anti-Utopians.* New York: Oxford University Press, 1967.

Holmes, Charles M. *Aldous Huxley and the Way to Reality.* Bloomington, Indiana: Indiana University Press, 1970.

Huxley, Julian, ed. *Aldous Huxley, 1894-1963: A Memorial Volume.* London: Chatto & Windus, 1965.

Huxley, Laura Archera. *This Timeless Moment: A Personal View of Aldous Huxley.* New York: Farrar, Straus & Giroux, 1968.

Meckier, Jerome. *Aldous Huxley: Satire and Structure.* London: Chatto & Windus, 1969.

O'Faolain, Sean. *The Vanishing Hero.* New York: Grosset & Dunlap, 1956.

Savage, Derek. *The Withered Branch: Six Studies in the Modern Novel.* London: Eyre & Spottiswoode, 1950.

Watts, Harold H. *Aldous Huxley.* New York: Twayne Publishers, Inc. 1969.

Webster, Harvey Curtis. *After the Trauma: Representative British Novelists Since 1920.* Lexington: University Press of Kentucky, 1970.
Woodcock, George. *Dawn and the Darkest Hour: A Study of Aldous Huxley.* New York: Viking Press, 1972.